The New York Times Style Book
for Writers and Editors

The New York Times

STYLE BOOK

for writers and editors

Edited and Revised by LEWIS JORDAN
News Editor, *The New York Times*

McGRAW-HILL BOOK COMPANY, INC.
NEW YORK   TORONTO   LONDON

The New York Times Style Book for Writers and Editors

46365

Foreword

Style book "style" does not mean literary style. It means, essentially, a set of rules or guides designed to assure consistency of spelling, capitalization, punctuation and abbreviation in printing the written word.

Why are rules necessary? Other things being equal, or at least in correct proportion, there is not much difference between a Martini and a martini. But a publication that capitalizes the word on one page and lower-cases it on another may lead the careful reader to believe that such untidiness extends to larger matters.

Style for a newspaper was no problem in the days when one man owned it, wrote it, edited it and printed it. By doing things his own way, he achieved consistency, whether he sought it or not. When dozens, or hundreds do the writing, editing and printing, a kind of anarchy will arise unless there are rules for all to follow.

If style rules do no more than call attention to the need for precision in writing, they must inevitably improve it and thus open the way to clear communication. A piece of writing that is properly spelled and properly punctuated is off to a good start.

This Style Book has been compiled for those who write, edit and print The New York Times. As a desk manual designed for quick reference, it cannot provide the answer to every question of style that may come up. Sometimes the an-

swer may be reached by analogy. For example, if a word or a class of words listed in the Style Book is capitalized, it is reasonable to capitalize similar words that are not listed.

The book is self-indexing. A boldface word or phrase that appears in the separate and alphabetical listings but is not discussed should be so spelled and capitalized in a normal sentence. Compound words are listed under the prefixes and suffixes with which they are formed. Abbreviations are listed separately, followed by the spelled-out forms. These listings are not intended to encourage the use of abbreviations, which in profusion are unsightly, but are given for the sake of easy reference. Titles of all sorts appear separately, rather than by categories and the forms for first and subsequent references are shown by example. A title that is abbreviated before a name is listed under the abbreviations. General subjects are also listed alphabetically, with cross references to separate, specific listings.

Webster's New International Dictionary, Second Edition, is followed for spelling and usage. But for spellings and definitions of new words, particularly in the fields of science, Webster's Third New International Dictionary is used. The authority for the spelling of geographic names is the Columbia Lippincott Gazetteer of the World. Any references in the Style Book to "the dictionary" or "the gazetteer" are to these authorities. In cases of conflict, the forms listed in the Style Book take precedence.

Two major changes in Times style should be noted. The first is the dropping of the foreign equivalents of Mr., Mrs. and Miss. This change, which follows a similar change in the State Department's Diplomatic List, was made because of the increasing difficulty of using foreign equivalents in a consistent manner. (See **Mr., Mrs., Miss.**) The second change is in the style for numbers. Instead of spelling out numbers up to 100, only the numbers one through nine will be spelled out in ordinary reading matter. (See **numbers.**)

Not all of the other changes in style can be listed here, but they include the following: the umlaut will be used in German words requiring it (see **accent marks**); *theatre* becomes *theater*; *Peiping* becomes *Peking*; *Communism* (which see) is now usually capitalized; several of the abbreviations for enlisted men's ranks have been changed (see separate listings).

Ideally, a set of style rules should be extensive enough to establish the desired system of style, but not so extensive as to inhibit the writer or the editor. The rules should encourage thinking, not discourage it. Ideally again, a single rule might suffice: "The rule of common sense will prevail at all times."

Contents

Style

A

a, an. The indefinite article *a* is used before words beginning with a consonant sound, including the aspirate *h*: *a car, a hotel, a historical.* It is also used before words like *union, euphonious, unit.* The indefinite article *an* is used before words beginning with a vowel sound: *onion, uncle, honor.*

The choice of article before an abbreviation or a symbol also depends upon the sound: *an 11-year-old boy, an N.Y.U. student.*

In a series, the article should appear before each of the coordinate nouns: *He was helped by a policeman, a fireman and a doctor. The hero and the heroine received medals.* An exception is made if the nouns convey a single idea: *He had a bow and arrow.*

See **articles** and **the.**

A.A. for Alcoholics Anonymous; also for an athletic association: *the Boston A.A.*

A.B. or **B.A.** for Bachelor of Arts. Also: *a bachelor's degree.*

abbreviations. Commonly used abbreviations are listed separately and alphabetically.

Points usually are used in abbreviations of the names of governmental bureaus and agencies, well-known organizations, companies, etc.: *F.C.C., N.A.M., A. & P.*

If an abbreviation has become a recognized word and is pronounced as a word, the points are omitted, although all the letters remain capitalized: *GATT, NATO, UNESCO, SEATO.* To avoid confusion, points are required in the cases of some abbreviations that spell actual words: *W.H.O., C.A.B.*

When letters within a single word are used as an abbreviation, they are capitalized but do not take points: *TB, TV.* But *V.D.* requires the points because it stands for two words.

Abbreviations may be used more freely in headlines than in stories. Certain titles spelled out in stories before last names may be contracted in heads: *Gen. Jones, Gov. Brown, Rep. Smith, etc.* Place designations also may be abbreviated in heads: *Fifth Ave., Fordham Rd., Patchen Pl.* But abbreviations like State *Dept.* and Ways and Means *Comm.* are not permitted in headlines.

Even freer use of abbreviations is permitted in tabular matter when it is necessary to conserve space and keep listings within one line as far as possible. In this case, *Dept.* and *Comm.* would be acceptable. All the standard abbreviations may be used, as well as coined contractions, provided, of course, that the item can be understood.

The main considerations in using abbreviations in stories and headlines are not to confuse the reader with any obscure contractions like *N.R.D.G.A.* (National Retail Dry Goods Association) and not to create a typographical mess by excessive use of abbreviations, which are often unsightly. There is no reason to inflict a sentence like this on the reader: *Earlier this year the P.M.A. reached agreements with the A.R.A., M.E.B.A., M.C.S. and S.I.U.*

A.B.C. for American Broadcasting Company.

A B C's.

able-bodied.

A-bomb may be used in stories as well as in headlines, but in both cases *atomic* or *atom bomb* is preferred. In upper-and-lower-case headlines, the *b* is capitalized: *A-Bomb*.

aboveboard.

A.C. for an athletic club: *the Manhattan A.C.*

academic degrees and titles. John P. Manley, Doctor of Philosophy (or Ph.D.); Prof. John P. Manley, Professor Manley, the professor. Degrees and titles are listed separately and alphabetically.

academic departments. Lower-case *department of natural history, department of English literature, etc.,* whether in school, college or university.

Academy. Capitalize in second references to the French Academy, the National Academy of Sciences and the United States Military, Naval and Air Force Academies: *the Academy.* But: *the service academies.*

a cappella.

accent marks. Six accents are to be used in ordinary reading matter in certain words of languages developed from the Latin and in German words. Some words have lost their accents through frequent use in English: *cafe, facade, etc.* Words that have lost their accents and words that require accents are listed separately and alphabetically. These include some exceptions to dictionary style, but in general the dictionary should be followed.

The most frequently used accents are the grave accent (*è*), the acute accent (*é*) and the circumflex (*â*): *arrière-pensée, raison d'être.*

The tilde (*ñ*), which in Spanish and Portuguese has a marked effect upon the pronunciation, should also be used when required: *vicuña, mañana, São Paulo.*

The cedilla (*ç*), used in French and other languages to denote a soft *c,* is also available and should be used in words requiring it: *garçon, François, français, etc.*

The German umlaut (*ü*), like the other accents, is to be used in stories but not in headlines. Normally, an *e* is added to the vowel when the umlaut is omitted. But to add an *e* in the head would create more of a discrepancy than would the absence of the umlaut. The difference between, say, *Düsseldorf* and *Dusseldorf* is so slight that any misunderstanding is unlikely. The slight disadvantage is outweighed by the advantage of more familiar spellings in stories: *Dürer, Tannhäuser.*

accommodate.

acknowledgment.

Acting. John P. Manley, Acting Secretary of State (and similar titles), the Acting Secretary.

acts and bills. Capitalize the titles of acts, bills and laws when the full official title is given or when the title by which the bill is generally known is used: *Social Security Act, Taft-Hartley Act, Multiple Dwelling Law.* But lower-case *bill* and *act* when standing alone or when used in shortened titles and general descriptive terms: *the housing bill, the security act.* Also lower-case *bill* when used with the sponsor's name unless the complete title is given: *the Smith bill, the Wagner bill.* But: *the Wagner Housing Bill.*

acute accent. See **accent marks.**

12

A.D. for anno Domini. In view of its meaning, the abbreviation is better placed before the year: *The town was founded A.D. 73.* Also because of its meaning, do not write *the fourth century A.D.* Put B.C. after the year: *The town was founded in 31 B.C.*

Addressograph (trademark).

Adjt. John P. Manley, Adjutant Manley, the adjutant.

Adjutant General. It is *Maj. Gen. John P. Manley, the Adjutant General,* when referring to the officer in charge of the Adjutant General's Corps of the United States Army. Also: Adjt. Gen. John P. Manley.

Adm. John P. Manley, Admiral Manley, the admiral.

Administration. Capitalize when referring to a specific Presidential administration of the United States Government: *the Kennedy Administration, the Administration.* Lowercase when referring to domestic state or city governments and to foreign governments of all kinds: *the Rockefeller administration, the Wagner administration, the Congo administration.*

Admiral of the Fleet John P. Manley, Admiral Manley (if the reference is to an American), the admiral. As a British rank, it cannot properly be shortened in second references. But British holders of the rank usually have other titles by which they can be called: *Admiral of the Fleet Earl Mountbatten of Burma, Earl Mountbatten, Lord Mountbatten.*

admissible.

adverb placement. An adverb used with a compound verb should nor-mally be placed between elements of the verb, as it is a few words back in this sentence and in the following example: *He will usually take the opposing side.* The split infinitive (which see) is another matter entirely.

adviser.

A.E.C. for Atomic Energy Commission.

aegis.

Aeroflot (Soviet airline).

Aerolineas Argentinas.

Aeronaves de Mexico.

Afghan hound.

A.F.L.-C.I.O. for American Federation of Labor and Congress of Industrial Organizations (which see).

African Methodist Episcopal Church.

African Methodist Episcopal Zion Church.

after-. afterbeat, afterdeck, after-dinner, aftereffect, aftermath, after-mentioned, after-theater, afterthought.

AFTRA for American Federation of Television and Radio Artists.

agenda. This may now be construed as a singular: *The agenda was adopted.*

ages. Use figures for ages of persons and animals: *John Smith, 25 years old; a 7-year-old boy; a race for 2-year-olds.* In a story giving the age of more than one person, use *years old* only with the first age given. In giving ages of inanimate objects or other things spell out through nine and use figures above nine: *two-year* *fight, a house eight years old, 10-year fight, a house 20 years old.*

ages and eras of history. Capitalize *Stone Age, Bronze Age, Iron Age, Dark Ages, Middle Ages, Renaissance, Age of Discovery, etc.,* but not *rocket age, atomic age, missile age, etc.*

aging.

"Aïda."

aide (assistant).

aide de camp.

air-. air-borne, air-condition, air-conditioned, air-conditioner, air-conditioning, aircrew, airdrop, airfield, airfreight, airlift (n., v., adj.), airline, airmail (n., v., adj.), airman, air-minded, airplane, air-raid (adj.), airship, airspace, airtight. But: air base, air express, air force, air raid (n.).

Air Chief Marshal Sir John Manley, Sir John, Air Chief Marshal Manley. This and other British Royal Air Force ranks cannot properly be shortened.

Airedale terrier.

Air Force. Capitalize in *United States Air Force, Royal Air Force, Soviet Air Force, etc.* It is *the Air Force* in subsequent references to that of the United States, but lowercase such references to any foreign air force. It is also *Air Force* in references to United States Air Force Academy sports teams.

Air Force Academy, the Academy.

Air France.

Air-India.

airline(s). But follow the lines' style

in proper names: *United Air Lines, American Airlines.* Lines are listed separately and alphabetically.

Airman John P. Manley, Airman Manley, the airman. Also: Airman 1st Cl. (or 2d or 3d Cl.) John P. Manley, Airman Manley, the airman.

Air National Guard.

airplane names. Do not quote them.

Ala. for Alabama after cities and towns.

à la carte.

Alaska. Do not abbreviate after cities and towns.

Alberta (Canadian province). Do not abbreviate after cities and towns.

albino, albinos.

Alitalia Airlines.

Allegany. Counties in New York and Maryland.

Alleghany. County in Virginia.

Alleghany Corporation.

Allegheny. This is the spelling for the mountains and for the river, city and county in Pennsylvania. The plural for Allegheny Mountains is Alleghenies, an exception to the rule that makes Germanys the plural of Germany.

Allegheny Airlines.

allies, allied. Do not capitalize in references to post-World War II alliances, including the alliance of the United States, Canada and the West European powers. The members of the North Atlantic Treaty Organization are *NATO allies, Western allies* or, if the context has been established, *allies.* There are also

CENTO allies and *SEATO allies*. Capitalize *Allies* and *Allied* in references to the World War I and World War II alliances and any similar alliance whose primary name includes *Allies* or *Allied*.

allot, allotting.

all right (never *alright*).

all-time. As an adjective applied to sports, weather and other records it is imprecise and superfluous.

allude, refer. To allude to something is to speak of it without direct mention; to refer is to mention directly.

alma mater.

almanacs. Do not quote their titles; capitalize principal words.

Alsatian wolfdog.

alumna (f.), **alumnae** (f. pl.), **alumnus** (m.), **alumni** (m. pl.).

A.M. (time). Capitalize: *10:30 A.M. yesterday.* Avoid this redundancy: *10:30 A.M. yesterday morning.* Also: *10 A.M.,* not *10:00 A.M.*

A.M.A. for American Medical Association.

Ambassador, ambassadorial. Ambassador John P. Manley; John P. Manley, Ambassador to Ceylon; the Ambassador. But: *a school for training ambassadors, an ambassador of goodwill,* etc. Lower-case *ambassadorial.*

Ambassador at Large. No hyphens. Capitalize when referring to a specific person holding a governmental position so titled.

amendments to the Constitution. Capitalize when referring to a specific amendment: *Fifth Amendment.*

Spell out ordinals through the ninth and use figures for 10th and above: *First Amendment, 14th Amendment.*

America, American(s), Americas. America is not only the United States but also North America or South America. Although citizens of the United States are not the only Americans, the word is generally reserved for them. But the words America, American and Americans may be used in all their senses if the context makes the meaning clear. The countries of the Western Hemisphere are, collectively, the Americas.

American Airlines.

American Baptist Convention.

American Export Lines.

American Federation of Labor and Congress of Industrial Organizations (A.F.L.-C.I.O.). This is the formal name of the merged labor movement and should be used at least once in every story concerning it. The abbreviation may be used in first references if necessary to avoid a cumbersome sentence.

American Geographical Society. Do not confuse with the National Geographic Society.

American President Lines.

American Stock Exchange.

American Telephone and Telegraph Company (A.T. & T.).

America's Cup (yachting), **Americas Cup** (golf).

amid (not *amidst*).

amidships.

among (not *amongst*).

15

ampersand (&). The ampersand may be used in some company names: *Baltimore & Ohio Railroad (B. & O.), Newport News Shipbuilding & Drydock Company, Price & Co., etc.* It should not otherwise be used in place of *and* in either stories or headlines. See **company and corporation names.**

AMVETS for American Veterans of World War II and Korea.

an. See **a, an.**

anemia, anemic.

anesthetic.

Anglo-. Anglo-Saxon, Anglo-American, Anglo-Catholic, Anglo-Indian. But: Anglophile, Anglophobia.

animals. Do not use personal pronouns in referring to animals unless their sex has been established or they have been personalized with names: *The dog was lost; it howled. Rover was lost; he howled. The dog, which was lost, howled. Rover, who was lost, howled. The bull tossed his horns.* Ages of animals are given in figures: *a race for 3-year-olds.*

Ankara (not *Angora*).

Ann Arbor Railroad.

ANTA for American National Theater and Academy.

Antarctic (n., adj.), Antarctic Circle, Antarctic Continent, Antarctica.

ante-. antebellum, antepenult. But: ante-Babylonian, ante-eternity.

anti-. antiaircraft, antislavery, antisocial, antitrust. But: anti-American, anti-Freud, Antichrist (an exception).

any-. anybody (pron.), anyhow,

anyone, anyway (in any event), anywhere. But: any way (not concerned in any way).

A. & P. for Great Atlantic and Pacific Tea Company.

apostle(s). Generally lower-case: *the apostles of Jesus, an apostle, the apostle.* But: *the Twelve Apostles, the Apostle Thomas, the Apostles' Creed.*

Apostolic Delegate. Capitalize when used with a name or when standing alone if the reference is to a specific individual. An apostolic delegate is a Roman Catholic representative accredited by the Pope to the church or hierarchy in a foreign country. He is not a nuncio, who is accredited to a foreign government.

apostrophe. The apostrophe is used to indicate the possessive case of nouns (*man's*), to denote a contraction or omission of letters (*it's* for *it is*, *'64* for *1964*), and to form the plurals of letters and symbols (*p's and q's, size 7's, B-52's*).

The singular possessive is formed with *'s* (*boy's coat*) and the plural with *s'* (*boys' coat, the Kennedys' car*).

Almost all singular words ending in *s* require another *s* as well as the apostrophe to form the possessive: *Dulles's, James's, Charles's, The Times's.* However, the *s* after the apostrophe is dropped when two or more sibilant sounds precede the apostrophe: *Kansas' Governor, Moses' behalf.* It is also dropped in certain expressions in which the word following the apostrophe begins with *s*: *for conscience' sake, for appearance' sake.*

The apostrophe is used when *Mc* or *Mac* occurs in a name in a headline or signature set in upper case: *M'CLELLAN, M'ARTHUR, etc.* If the setting is upper and lower case or caps and small caps, use *c* and *ac.*

Apostrophes are omitted in names of many organizations: *Citizens Union, Doctors Hospital, Teachers College, etc.* But if the word is plural before the addition of an *s*, the apostrophe is used: *Young Men's Christian Association, Children's Court.*

In contractions that have come into common usage, the apostrophe is not used: *cello, cellist, copter, chutist, phone, plane.* The apostrophe is used in abbreviations and contractions like *O.K.'d.*

appall.

Appellate Division.

April. Do not abbreviate.

aquavit (not *akvavit*).

Arab names are usually Arab words governed by grammatical rules. Many of them incorporate the definite article *al.* The vowel may appear as *a, e* or *u*, or disappear entirely as a result of elision. The *l* may appear as *d, dh, n, r, s, sh, t, th* or *z.* The definite article may be joined with the preceding or the following word, or both. Except where other usage has become established (Abdel Nasser, Abdullah) use *al* hyphenated with the following word: al-Sabah, al-Azhar. Many Arabs prefer to drop the definite article from their names in English: Mamoun Kuzbari, not *al-Kuzbari.*

Compound names should be left intact. The commonest are composed with the word *Abd* (Worshiper of): Abdullah (Worshiper of God), Abdel Nasser (Worshiper of the Vic-

torious One), Abdur Rahman (Worshiper of the Merciful One). The use of Nasser alone in second references to Gamal Abdel Nasser, although wrong, is established.

Another compound is completed by *al-Din* (the Religion), which may appear in such forms as *ed-Din, eddine, uddin, etc.*: Kamal ed-Din (the Perfection of the Religion), Nureddin (the Light of the Religion), Allah-ud-Din or Aladdin (the God of the Religion).

Allah or *ullah* (God) completes such compound names as Jad-Allah (God giveth), Nasrullah (the Victory of God). *Abu* (Father of) and *Ibn, bin* or *ben* (Son of) combine in such names as Abulhuda, Abubakr, Abul Zalaf, Ibn Saud. Do not capitalize *ibn* when it is preceded by first or middle names.

Moslem Arabs have at least three names—their own given name, their father's given name and their grandfather's given name. The permanent family name, if there is one, follows. Use whichever family name the subject himself seems to prefer. Otherwise, in second references prefix *Mr.* or the official title to the last name and treat it as a family name. When in doubt, repeat the name in full in second references.

The Arab titles Pasha and Bey, both of Turkish origin, have been abolished. Royal titles, as in English, are used with the first name: Emir (Prince) Faisal ibn Abd al-Aziz al-Saud, Emir Faisal. Sheik (Elder, Patriarch, Religious Leader) is the title of the rulers of the Persian Gulf principalities: Sheik Abdullah al-Salim al-Sabah, Sheik Abdullah. The title and the first name alone suffice in first references to rulers (kings, imams, emirs and sheiks) unless it is necessary to give the full name to distinguish between two persons with the same title and the same first name.

Haj (Pilgrim) is used with the first name in first and second references: Haj Amin al-Husseini, Haj Amin.

Arabic terms in place names include the following: Ain (spring), Bab (gate), Bahr (sea, lake and sometimes river), Bir (well), Birket (pond), Burj (tower), Dahr (mountaintop), Dar (abode of), Deir (monastery), Jebel (mountain), Jisr (bridge), Kafr (hamlet), Khan (caravanserai), Marj (meadow), Nahr (river), Naqb (pass), Qasr or Kasr (castle), Ras (promontory, peak), Tell (hill), Wadi (valley, ravine).

In Egyptian usage, the standard Arabic *j* is pronounced as a hard *g*. Thus Burg, Gebel, Gisr and Marg appear in Egyptian place names instead of Burj, Jebel, Jisr and Marj.

French modes of transliteration have become standard usage for North African names; thus Djebel and Ouadi instead of Jebel and Wadi. But in all cases the gazetteer spelling is to be used.

arch-. archangel, archbishop (which see), archdeacon, archdiocese, archduke, archenemy, archfiend. But: arch-Protestant, arch-Republican.

Archbishop. *The Most Rev. John P. Manley, Archbishop of, etc.*, is the proper form for the Roman Catholic Church and the Church of England. Also: *the Archbishop*. See **Bishop.**

archeology. Also: archeological, archeologist.

Arctic (n., adj.). Arctic Circle, Arctic Ocean, Arctic Current, Arctic zone, arctics (overshoes).

Argentines. The people of Argentina. The adjective is *Argentine*.

Ariz. for Arizona after cities and towns.

Ark. for Arkansas after cities and towns.

Armed Forces Day.

Armenian Church of America, Diocese.

Armistice Day (Nov. 11) is now Veterans Day in the United States.

Army. Capitalize in *United States Army, British Army, Soviet Army, etc.* It is *the Army* in subsequent references to the United States Army, but lower-case such references to any foreign army. It is also *Army* in reference to United States Military Academy sports teams.

Army corps. A United States Army corps is designated by Roman numerals: *XVI Corps*.

Army ranks are listed separately and alphabetically.

articles. See **a, an** and **the.** Avoid the faddish practice of dropping *A* and *The* when they begin a sentence. If several consecutive paragraphs of a story begin with the same article, recast enough of the first sentences of the paragraphs to break up the monotony.

ASCAP for American Society of Composers, Authors and Publishers.

Asian, Asiatic. Use the noun *Asian* or *Asians* when referring to people. *Asiatic*, in this sense, is regarded by some Asians as offensive.

as much as. *As much as if not more than;* not, *as much if not more than.*

Assembly. Capitalize in *United Nations General Assembly, the State Assembly, etc.* In second references: *the Assembly.* But it is *state assembly, state assemblies, an assembly, etc.,* when the reference is not specific.

Assembly districts. Capitalize in specific references: *First Assembly District, 11th Assembly District.*

Assemblyman John P. Manley, the Assemblyman.

assistant. Some subordinate titles containing the word *assistant* are not capitalized, except before names, in references to specific individuals: *The assistant district attorney spoke briefly.* This applies especially in cases where the subordinate rank is shared by several persons. However, it does not apply at all to positions of major importance: *the Assistant Secretary of State.* See **deputy.**

Associate Justice John P. Manley (of the Supreme Court of the United States), the Associate Justice, the Justice.

Associated Press, The. It is *The Associated Press* in stories. *A.P.* is the abbreviation, except in datelines: RECIFE, Brazil, June 10 (AP)—etc. Use a centered agate credit line above the dateline on Page 1 stories:
By The Associated Press

association. Capitalize when part of the name of an organization, but not in second references. Also capitalize in *Association football* (British).

Atchison, Topeka & Santa Fe Railway, the Santa Fe.

Atlantic. The actual shoreline of the Atlantic Ocean is the Atlantic *coast;* the region of the United States lying along the shoreline is the Atlantic *Coast* or the Atlantic *Seaboard.* It is *the coast* in all second references. Only the West Coast is referred to as *the Coast.* Also: *North Atlantic, South Atlantic, Atlantic Coast States.*

Atlantic Coast Line Railroad, the Coast Line.

at large. Do not hyphenate *ambassador at large, councilman at large, delegate at large, representative at large.* Capitalize in all references to a person holding a governmental position that has *at large* in its title: *John P. Manley, Councilman at Large.*

atomic age.

A.T. & T. for American Telephone and Telegraph Company.

attaché. Col. John P. Manley, military attaché; the attaché.

Attorney General John P. Manley, the Attorney General. Plural: *attorneys general.*

Aug. for August before numerals: *Aug. 16.*

autobahn (sing.), **autobahns** (pl.).

automatic pistol. This hand weapon, designed for automatic or semiautomatic firing, is not a revolver. The automatic's cartridges are held in a magazine, the revolver's in chambers in a cylinder that revolves. Both are properly called pistols.

automobile racing and rallies. Times of races are given in figures: *His time was 2 hours 13 minutes, an average speed of 97 miles an hour.*

Many racing cars are variations

of models sold by automobile dealers. The variations should be specified: *Cooper Climax, birdcage Maserati, 1961 Ford with a 1957 Thunderbird engine, etc.* Grand prix races are usually conducted for cars similar in engine size. These sizes are known as formulas: *Formula One, Formula Junior, Formula Libre, etc.*

In auto rallies, drivers must cover specified road courses at specified speeds. Such events should not be referred to as races.

autumn (also *fall*).

Ave. may be used for *Avenue* in headlines with the names of avenues.

avenues. See **streets and avenues.**

Avianca (Colombian National Airways).

awe-struck.

a while, awhile. *He plans to stay for a while. He plans to stay awhile.*

ax.

Axis. The German-Italian-Japanese alliance of World War II.

B

baby-sit, baby-sitting, baby sitter.

baccalaureate.

back(-), -back. backache, backbone, backfield, backfire, background, backhand, backlog, back room (n.), back-room (adj.), back seat (n.), back-seat (adj.), back stairs (n.), backstairs (adj.), backstop, backstretch, backstroke, backwoods. Also (all n.): comeback, flareback, halfback, setback, switchback, throwback.

Baghdad.

baked alaska.

ball-bearing.

Baltimore & Ohio Railroad, the B. & O.

Band-Aid (trademark).

Bangor & Aroostook Railroad.

banknote.

bar-. barkeeper, barmaid, barman, barroom, bartender.

Barbados.

bar mitzvah.

Baron. Lord, not Baron, is the customary form in Britain: *Lord Beaverbrook.* In other foreign countries, Baron is used.

baseball. Scores are given in figures: *The Giants won, 12 to 6.* Numbers of runs, hits and innings below 10 are spelled out: *They scored three runs in the seventh inning. In the 10th inning, they got their 12th hit.* Capitalize *All-Star Game, World Series* and *Little World Series.*

Avoid tired words and phrases like *all-time, autumn classic, annex* (as a verb), *frame, hat trick, homer* (as a verb), *nightcap, Pale Hose, win* (as a noun), *winless, etc.*

Basel (Switzerland).

Basenji (dog).

basis, bases.

basketball. Use figures for points and scores: *He scored 8 points in two minutes. They won, 99 to 98.* Spell out the number of baskets below 10: *He made only four baskets in the first half, but shot 17 in the second.* Also: *24-second rule.*

bas-relief.

basset hound.

Bastille.

bath(-). bathhouse, bath mat, bathroom, bathtub, bath towel.

battalion. Capitalize in names: *Third Battalion.*

battle-. battle-ax, battlefield, battlefront, battleground, battleship.

bavarian cream (a dessert).

Bayreuth (Germany).

B.B.C. for British Broadcasting Corporation.

B.C. As an abbreviation for *before Christ* it follows the year: *The town was founded in 59 B.C.* In view of its meaning, *A.D.* is better placed before the year: *The town was founded A.D. 73.* Use *B.C.* also for boat club (*Schuylkill B.C.*) and for British Columbia after cities and towns.

beagle.

bed-. bedroom, bedside, bedspring.

Bedlington terrier.

Bedloes Island has been renamed Liberty Island.

Beirut (Lebanon).

Bellaire (L. I.).

Bellerose (L. I.).

Bellmore (L. I.).

benediction.

benefited, benefiting.

Benelux. Belgium, the Netherlands and Luxembourg.

Benzedrine (trade name).

Bering Sea.

Bermuda shorts.

Bermudian.

beside (at the side of).

besides (in addition to).

besiege.

bessemer converter.

best(-). best-dressed, best-informed, best-liked, best man, best-paid, best seller, best-selling.

bettor.

bi-. biangular, bicameral, bicentennial, bilateral, bilingual, bimonthly, bipartisan, bistate, biweekly, bizonal.

Bible Belt. Use with care because in certain contexts it can give offense.

Bible, Biblical. Capitalize if the reference is to the Old Testament or the New Testament. See **Scripture(s).**

Big Three (or *Four, Five, etc.*). Construe as a plural. Numerals may be used in headlines: *Big 3.*

bikini (two-piece bathing suit).

Bill of Rights.

bills (legislative). See **acts and bills.**

birdseye (adj.).

Bishop. In the Methodist Church, which has no prelates, it is *Bishop John P. Manley, the Bishop.* In the Lutheran and Protestant Episcopal Churches it is *the Right Rev. John P. Manley, Bishop of, etc.; the Bishop.* In the Roman Catholic Church it is *the Most Rev. John P. Manley, Bishop of, etc.; the Bishop.* See **Archbishop.**

bivouac, bivouacking.

black-. blackjack, blacklist, blackmail, blackout.

blame on. This is to be avoided: *The wreck was blamed on carelessness.* Since the wreck is not the target of the blame, it should be: *Carelessness was blamed for the wreck. The wreck was attributed to carelessness.*

blasé.

blitz, blitzkrieg.

blizzard. Do not call a storm a blizzard unless it meets the Weather Bureau's specifications: a violent, intensely cold wind laden with snow, mostly or entirely picked up from the ground; winds of at least 35 miles an hour; visibility reduced to 500 feet or less. A severe blizzard: wind of 45 miles an hour or more; temperature of 10 degrees or less; visibility near zero.

blockfront.

blond (n. m. and adj.), **blonde** (n. f.).

bloodhound.

blowout.

BMT for Brooklyn-Manhattan Transit.

board. Capitalize only when part of a name. Do not abbreviate, even in headlines.

Board of Regents, the Regents.

Boardwalk (Coney Island, Atlantic City).

boat-. boathook, boathouse, boatload, boatman. But: boat race.

bogey. One over par in golf (pl. *bogeys*). *Bogy* is a bugbear (pl. *bogies*).

bona fide.

bondholder.

book-. bookcase, bookkeeper, bookmaker, bookmark, bookseller, bookshelf, bookshop, bookstore.

Book of Common Prayer.

books. In ordinary matter, quote their titles and capitalize principal words.

boost. Avoid as a verb or a noun unless the context calls for a colloquialism or slang, or the subject is rocketry.

border terrier.

"Boris Godunov" (the opera).

Borough President John P. Manley, the Borough President.

borscht.

Börse (German exchange).

Bosporus, the (not *Bosporus Straits*).

Boston & Maine Railroad.

Boston Stock Exchange.

Boston terrier.

Boulevard. Spell out and capitalize in ordinary reading matter when part of a name: *Bruckner Boulevard.* The abbreviation *(Bruckner Blvd.)* may be used in headlines and in agate and other special matter.

bound-, -bound. eastbound, northbound, snowbound. But: Africa-bound, vacation-bound.

Bourse (French exchange).

boutonniere.

bowl games. Capitalize: *Rose Bowl, Cotton Bowl, Orange Bowl,* etc.

box(-). box car, box office (n.), box-office (adj.), box kite, boxlike, box spring (n.), box-spring (adj.).

boxing. Spell out the number of rounds below 10 and use figures for the time within a round: *2:03 of the sixth round.* Also use figures for the knockdown count: *a count of 8.* In all stories, even those of one paragraph, give the fighters' weights and their home towns.

Boy Scout, a Scout, the Scouts.

brackets. See **parentheses and brackets.**

brand-new.

Braniff Airways.

brazil nut.

break-. breakdown (n.), breakoff (n.), breakthrough (n.), breakup (n.), breakwater.

breast-stroke.

breechloader.

bribetaker.

bric-a-brac.

bridge. See **contract bridge.**

briefcase.

Brig. John P. Manley, Brigadier Manley, the brigadier.

Brig. Gen. John P. Manley, General Manley, the general.

British European Airways.

British Overseas Airways Corporation, B.O.A.C.

British titles are listed separately and alphabetically.

Briton (not *Britisher*).

broadcast (never *broadcasted*).

broad jump.

Bronze Age.

Brookings Institution.

Brooklyn Heights, the Heights.

Brooklyn Navy Yard may be used in stories and headlines instead of the official name, New York Naval Shipyard. The official name should be worked into stories occasionally when it can be done gracefully.

Bros. for Brothers in some company names. See **company and corporation names.**

Brünnhilde.

brussels carpet.

Brussels griffon (dog).

brussels sprouts.

B.S. for Bachelor of Science.

Budapest.

building names. Capitalize the names of governmental buildings, churches, office buildings, hotels, especially designated rooms, etc.: *Criminal Court Building, First Presbyterian Church, Empire State Building, Commodore Hotel, Grand Central Terminal, Persian Room, Sing Sing Prison.*

bulldog, bullterrier.

bullet. It is the bullet, not the cartridge, that is discharged from the muzzle of a gun. The cartridge is a case that contains an explosive charge and the bullet before firing.

bullseye.

bunsen burner.

bureau. Capitalize when part of a name: *Bureau of Indian Affairs.* But: *the Washington bureau of The Times.* Do not abbreviate, even in headlines.

burglarize. Do not use.

burglary, robbery, theft. Burglary must involve breaking and entering. Robbery is stealing from a person or persons or from his or their presence. Theft is the act of stealing, usually carried out by stealth or in secrecy.

Burmese names. Many Burmese have only one name. However, many Burmese names begin with titles of honor, status, endearment, etc. U, for example, means uncle, while Thakin means master. Such a title is used with the name in the first reference: *U Nu*, or *Premier U Nu*. In second references it is *Premier Nu* or *Mr. Nu*. In the case of Burmese who have more than one name, the names are used in second as well as first references: *U Tin Maung, Mr. Tin Maung*.

bus, buses.

business directories and guides. Do not quote their titles; capitalize principal words.

businessman, businesswoman. But: *small-business man.* See **compound words.**

by-. by-election, byline, bylaw, bypass (n., v.), bypath, byplay, by-product, byroad, bystander, byword.

bylines. In the news sections, bylines are to be set as follows, in boldface caps:

By JOHN P. MANLEY

When a description of the author is included, the byline is set as follows:

By HOWARD TAUBMAN
New York Times Drama Critic

Except for the differences in type, the style is similar for the Book Review, Magazine and other sections.

C

C.A.B. for Civil Aeronautics Board.

Cabinet should be capitalized when the reference is to a specific national council: *The British Cabinet met. He was reappointed to the Cabinet.*

cabinet lists are set hanging indent in 8 point or 6½ point:

> *Premier*—Francisco Largo Caballero, Socialist.
> *Agriculture*—Vincent Uribe, Communist.
> *Air and Marine*—Indalecio Prieto, Socialist.
> *Foreign*—Julio Alvarez del Vayo, Socialist.
> *Interior*—Angel Galarza, Socialist.
> *Public Works* — José Antonio Aguirre, Basque Nationalist.

cabinet titles, both United States and foreign, are capitalized: Secretary of Labor John P. Manley, Minister of Justice, etc.; the Secretary, the Minister.

Cadet John P. Manley, Cadet Manley, the cadet.

caddie (golf).

cafe.

Cairn terrier.

caliber (of guns). Figures and abbreviations (if the measure is metric) are used in giving the calibers of guns: *.22 rifle, .38-caliber revolver, .410-gauge shotgun* (the only shotgun so measured), *7.3-inch gun, 11-inch cannon, 8-pound gun, 8-pounder, 110-mm. gun.* Shotguns, except for the .410, are not measured in inches: *10-gauge shotgun, 12-gauge, etc.*

Calif. for California after cities and towns.

cameraman.

Canada (not *Dominion of Canada*).

Canadian National Railways.

Canadian Press, The. It is *The Canadian Press* in stories. The abbreviation *C.P.* is not used. Dateline style is: WINDSOR, Canada, June 12 (Canadian Press)—etc. Use a centered agate credit line above the dateline on Page 1 stories:

By The Canadian Press

Canadian Pacific Airlines.

Canadian Pacific Railway.

Canadian Pacific Steamships.

Canadian provinces. Abbreviations of their names used after towns and cities are listed separately and alphabetically.

Canal is capitalized in second reference to the Panama Canal only.

Canal Zone (Panama) is abbreviated (*C.Z.*) after the names of cities and towns.

cancel, canceled, canceling, cancellation.

candle-, candlelight, candlestick, candle power.

cannot.

cantaloupe.

canto, cantos.

canvas (cloth), **canvass** (to solicit).

Cape Breton Island. Do not abbreviate after cities and towns.

Capetown (South Africa).

capital (of country or state). Lower-case *capital, national capital, state capital, the capital city; Trenton, the capital of New Jersey.*

capitalization. Style for capitalization is given throughout the book in the separate and alphabetical listings. A word, phrase or abbreviation that is listed but not discussed is to be used in a normal sentence as it appears, capitalized or not capitalized, in the listing.

In upper-and-lower-case headlines, capitalize nouns, pronouns and verbs, and all other words of four or more letters. Capitalize *No, Nor, Not, Off, Out, So, Up, etc.* Lower-case *a, and, as, at, but, by, for, if, in, of, on, or, the, to,* except when they appear at the beginnings of lines in the tops of heads, at the beginnings of banks, and following dashes in banks. Some of the foregoing words also are capitalized when connected with the preceding word, as in *Mayor Drops In* and *Cared For by His Mother.* Set infinitive as follows: *to Be, to Do, to Go, etc.* Capitalize both words of a compound adjective: *Able-Bodied Citizen.* Lower-case after hyphen in numbers (*One-tenth, Twenty-two*) and in words like *Re-elect, Co-worker, etc.* Always capitalize the first word of the second or third line of a headline. Capitalize the principal words in the headings of tables, lists, etc., in tabular matter.

Capitol. Capitalize all references to a specific national or state building. Also: *Capitol Hill, the Hill.*

Capt. John P. Manley, Captain Manley, the captain. This applies to military, naval, maritime and police captains.

carat, karat. The weight of precious

25

stones, especially diamonds, is expressed in carats. The proportion of pure gold used with an alloy is expressed in karats.

carburetor.

Cardinal. John Cardinal Manley, Cardinal Manley, the Cardinal. The first name may be dropped in first references to the Cardinal of the New York Archdiocese.

care-. carefree, caretaker, careworn.

CARE for Cooperative for American Relief Everywhere.

caret (writers' and proofreaders' mark).

cargo, cargoes.

Caribbean Sea.

carload.

Carnegie Institute (Pittsburgh).

Carnegie Institution (Washington).

carte blanche.

cartridge. A cartridge for a gun is a case that contains an explosive charge and a bullet or shot. The gun discharges only the bullet or shot.

cashmere (wool).

casket. Do not use in referring to the box in which a corpse lies. Use *coffin* instead.

caster (roller).

cast-off (n.).

castor (oil).

casualty lists are set hanging indent in 6½ point, with a full-measure 8-point italic introduction. The last name is given first in light caps, and

the names are alphabetized. Use P heads or G caps for categories.

Following is a list of the dead and injured in yesterday's plane crash:

Dead

ROE, Richard, 22 years old, Garden Grove, Calif.

Injured

DOE, John, 48, Los Angeles, the pilot.

In lists in which street addresses are included, clearly understood abbreviations like Ave., Blvd., St. and Sq. may be used.

catalogue.

catboat. A sailboat having one mast, far forward, and one sail.

catcall.

catchup (not *catsup* or *ketchup*).

Cathedral Church of St. John the Divine.

Catholic. It does not necessarily mean *Roman Catholic*. If that is meant, use *Roman Catholic* in all first references and in subsequent references also if necessary to avoid confusion.

cause célèbre.

cave-in (n.).

C.B.S. for Columbia Broadcasting System.

cedilla. See **accent marks.**

cellist, cello.

cement. There are many kinds of cement, which is a binding agent. One kind is among the ingredients of the artificial stone called concrete. Thus: *The wall was built with concrete* (not *cement*) *blocks.*

center-. centerboard, centerpiece. But: center field.

center around. Avoid the expression. Use *center on, center in* or *revolve around*.

Centerport (L. I.).

CENTO for Central Treaty Organization.

Central Conference of American Rabbis. A Reform group.

Central of Georgia Railway.

Central Railroad Company of New Jersey, the Jersey Central.

central standard time (C.S.T.).

Centre Street.

cents. See **dollars and cents.**

centuries. Lower-case and spell out through the ninth: *the eighth century, the 12th century.* Hyphenate in adjective form: *18th-century poet.* See **years.**

Chamber of Deputies, the Chamber.

Champs-Elysées.

characters in books, plays, etc. Do not quote their names: *He played Hotspur.*

chargé d'affaires.

chassis (sing. and pl.).

chateau.

chef-d'oeuvre.

chemical elements and formulas. Do not capitalize the names of the elements, even when used with the atomic numbers: *carbon 14, strontium 90, uranium 235.* Chemical formulas are set thus: H_2O, CO_2.

Chesapeake & Ohio Railway, the C. & O.

chess. Chess terms, unless they include proper names, should be lower-case: *Ruy Lopez opening, Philidor's defense, king's bishop's gambit, queen's gambit declined, giuoco pi-*ano opening. Never capitalize names of the pieces—king, queen, bishop, knight, rook (or castle), pawn—but when moves are given by initials, set thus: K–Kt3, Kt–K6, K–R, K–R sq, P(Kt2)xP, KxB, Q–Kt8, ch., etc.

chesterfield (overcoat).

Chiang Kai-shek.

Chicago Board of Trade.

Chicago, Burlington & Quincy Railroad, the Burlington.

Chicago & Eastern Illinois Railroad.

Chicago Great Western Railway, the Great Western.

Chicago Mercantile Exchange.

Chicago, Milwaukee, St. Paul & Pacific Railroad, the Milwaukee.

Chicago & North Western Railway, the North Western.

Chicago, Rock Island & Pacific Railroad, the Rock Island.

Chief Justice John P. Manley, the Chief Justice. It is Chief Justice *of the United States,* not *of the Supreme Court.*

Chief of Staff. Gen. John P. Manley, Chief of Staff; the Chief of Staff.

Chief Petty Officer John P. Manley, Mr. (or Chief Petty Officer) Manley, the chief petty officer.

Chief Warrant Officer John P. Manley, Mr. (or Chief Warrant Officer) Manley, the chief warrant officer.

chinaware.

Chinese names. A modified form of the Wade-Giles system is to be used in the transliteration of Chinese names. The apostrophes that are part of this system are not to be used: Chiang *Kai*-shek, not *K'ai*-shek. Note that the name following the hyphen is not capitalized. In Chinese names, the family name usually comes first: *Chiang* in a second reference to Chiang Kai-shek. Some Chinese have westernized their names, putting their given names or the initials for them first: *Dr. Tsing-fu Tsiang, K.C. Wu.*

chinese red (color).

chit-chat.

chock-full.

choirmaster.

chord (music, mathematics).

chow chow (dog).

Christ. See Jesus.

Christian Methodist Episcopal Church.

Christian Science. The name of the church organization is the Church of Christ, Scientist. Its principal church, in Boston, is the Mother Church.

The church has practitioners, lecturers and readers. These titles are capitalized only before a name: *Reader John P. Manley; John P. Manley, reader.* Never use *Rev.*

Christmas. Never abbreviate to *Xmas* or any other form.

church. Capitalize when used in the name of an organization or a building: *Protestant Episcopal Church, Roman Catholic Church, First Presbyterian Church, etc.* In second references: *the church.*

church and state. Do not capitalize when used in this sense: *conflict between church and state, church-state issue.*

churchgoer.

Church of Christ, Scientist. See **Christian Science.**

Church of Jesus Christ of Latter-day Saints. See **Mormon.**

Church of the Brethren.

churches and other religious organizations are listed separately and alphabetically.

Churches of Christ.

chute (parachute), chutist.

C.I.A. for Central Intelligence Agency.

cigarette.

circumflex. See accent marks.

City, city. Capitalize *New York City* and *City of New York* as official names; otherwise lower-case: *the city of Chicago, the city of Boston.* Also: *the city, the city government.* Capitalize *City* when used with the name of an official agency or with an official title: *the City Planning Commission, City Controller John P. Manley.*

City Council, the Council.

City of London (financial district), the City.

citywide.

Ciudad Trujillo is Santo Domingo again.

claptrap.

class-. classmate, classroom. But: class day. Also: *class of 1943* (or *'43*).

clean-. clean-cut, cleanup (n.).

clear-. clear-cut, clear-eyed, clear-minded.

clerical titles are listed separately and alphabetically.

cliché.

clientele.

climax. Do not use as a verb.

clock time. See time.

clockwise, counterclockwise.

close-up (n., adj.).

closure (not *cloture*).

clubhouse.

club officers. Do not capitalize titles.

clue.

clumber spaniel.

co-. co-author, co-defendant, coed, coeducation, coequal, coexist, coexistence, co-op, cooperate, cooperation, cooperative (n., adj.), coordinate, coordination, co-owner, co-partner, co-pilot, co-star, co-worker.

Co. for Company in some names. See **company and corporation names.**

coast. Lower-case when referring to an actual shoreline: *Atlantic coast, Pacific coast, east coast, west coast, etc.* Capitalize when referring to certain specific regions of the United States lying along such shorelines: *Atlantic Coast, Pacific Coast, Gulf Coast, West Coast, East Coast.* Do not capitalize when reference is to lesser regions: *the Jersey coast.* Capitalize *Coast* standing alone only when the reference is to the West Coast.

Coast Guard (United States). Mem-bers are *coastguardsmen.* Capitalize only before a name: *Coastguardsman John P. Manley.*

Coca-Cola, Coke (trademarks).

cocker spaniel.

cocksure.

coconut.

c.o.d. for cash, or collect, on delivery.

codes. Lower-case *steel code, oil code, building code, etc.* Capitalize such titles as *Code of Civil Procedure, Penal Code, Code Napoléon.*

coffeehouse.

coffin. Use this word, not *casket,* for the box in which a corpse lies.

Col. John P. Manley, Colonel Manley, the colonel.

cold-blooded.

cold war.

collectible.

College of Cardinals.

Collegiate Reformed Church of St. Nicholas.

collide, collision. There is a collision only when both bodies are in motion. If the phrase *collided with* seems to fix blame, it can be avoided by using this construction: *An automobile and a bus collided.* The phrase *were in collision* accomplishes the same purpose, but is stilted and should be avoided.

collie.

colloquialisms. Use only when the context justifies them. Do not quote.

Colo. for Colorado after cities and towns.

colon. The colon is used as a mark of introduction to a word, phrase, sentence, passage, list, tabulation, text, textual excerpts, etc. It is also used in giving clock times (10:30 A.M.) and, in sports, the times of races (*2:55, 4:10:23*).

As a mark of punctuation within the sentence the colon can be effective: *Today is the dead center of the year, or as near dead center as one can conveniently get: 182 days gone by, 182 to come.*

In ordinary writing, the first word after a colon is not capitalized if what follows is not a complete sentence: *There were three considerations: expense, time and feasibility.* But: *He promised this: The company will make good all the losses.*

While a comma suffices to introduce a direct quotation of one sentence that remains within the paragraph, the colon should be used to introduce longer quotations.

Do not use a dash with a colon.

Colorado & Southern Railway.

color-blind.

combated, combating.

combined words are listed separately and alphabetically.

Comdr. John P. Manley, Commander Manley, the commander.

comeback (n.)

Comédie Française.

come to a head. Avoid as trite.

comma. Do not use a comma before *and* in a series unless the other elements of the series are separated by semicolons: *Automobiles, buses and trains were stalled. Jack Jones, the coach; Dick Smith, a player, and Harry Roberts, an umpire, were arrested.* But use a comma in sentences like this to avoid confusion: *A martini is made of gin and vermouth, and lemon peel may be added if desired.*

Commas also are to be used in compound sentences before *but* and *for*: *The track was slow, but the betting was fast. He was impatient, for his dismissal was due any day.* But: *The comma is small but mighty.*

Use commas to set off a nonrestrictive phrase: *The house, which was 100 years old, was still in good condition.* Do not use the comma after an identifying noun used in the restrictive sense: *The painter Van Gogh had a hard struggle.* The absence of commas in *His brother George was best man* means that the bridegroom has more than one brother. If there is only one brother, *George* should be set off by commas. Thus a monogamous society must be well supplied with commas: *His wife, Nancy, was not there.*

The comma may also be used to introduce a quotation: *He said, "I will be back."* For quotations of more than one sentence use the colon (which see).

In general, use the comma when giving figures in thousands (*1,250 miles, $12,416.22*). But do not use it in designations of years, street numbers, box numbers, room numbers or telephone numbers.

In financial matter, precise use of the comma is often needed to avoid confusion: *The stock advanced 3 points, to 21.* The comma makes it clear that the range of advance was not between 3 and 21, but from 18 upward.

Do not use a comma before an *of* indicating place or position: *George*

H. Brown of Brooklyn. President de Gaulle of France. In ages, distances, times, etc., expressed in the following form, the comma is omitted: *4 years 9 months 21 days; 2 hours 15 minutes 10 seconds.*

Parentheses are used instead of commas in constructions like these: *the Salem (Ore.) public schools, The Lima (Ohio) News.*

In attributing ordinary quoted matter, put the comma before the quotation mark: *"I am ready," he said.*

commander. See **Comdr.**

Commander in Chief. No hyphens. Capitalize in specific references.

commencement (academic).

commission. Capitalize only when part of a name. Do not abbreviate, even in headlines.

Commissioner John P. Manley, the Commissioner. This also applies to forms like *Police Commissioner.*

commitment.

committee. Capitalize only when part of a name. Do not abbreviate, even in headlines.

Commodity Exchange.

common-. commonplace, commonweal, commonwealth.

Common Market. This unofficial designation for the European Economic Community may be used in first as well as in subsequent references, but the official name should be used at least once in every story.

communiqué.

communiqués are set in 8-point or

6½-point indent, with a full-measure 8-point italic introduction:

> *WASHINGTON, Jan. 10 (AP)— Navy communiqué 246:*
> On Jan. 8, during the forenoon, Marauder medium bombers (Martin B-26) with Airacobra (Bell P-39) escort bombed the Japanese airfield at Munda on New Georgia Island. Results were not reported.

Communism. Capitalize when referring to the Communist party movement and philosophy. Lower-case in a general sense: *The residents of Brook Farm sought to achieve communism.*

Communist. Capitalize as a noun for a member of the Communist party and as an adjective referring to the party or its philosophy.

company (military). Capitalize only when part of a name: *Company A, Company H, Service Company, the company.*

company and corporation names. In ordinary reading matter spell out Company, Corporation, Brothers, etc., in names when not directly preceded by an ampersand: *Brown Brothers, J. B. Mathews & Bros.; the H. S. Smith Company, Price & Co.* The ampersand also is used in personal firm names like these: *Blank & Stoller, Johnson & Murphy Company.*

The authority for the spelling of railroad names is the Association of American Railroads' listing, which uses the ampersand: *Baltimore & Ohio Railroad (B. & O.).* However, the ampersand is not used in many other names that also are descriptive: *American Telephone and Telegraph Company, Steel and Iron Products, Inc.* But it is often used in abbreviations of such names (*A.T.&T.*).

Company and corporation names —chiefly those of airlines, railroads and ship lines— are listed separately and alphabetically.

company officers. Do not capitalize titles: *He was elected president of the company. They complained to the president, John P. Manley.*

compound words are listed separately and alphabetically. To avoid confusion, and sometimes absurdities, compound nouns that are usually solid words should be separated when the first part of the compound is modified by an adjective: *businessman, small-business man; sailmaker, racing-sail maker.*

comptroller. Use *controller* instead.

concerto. Capitalize in a title: *Mozart's Piano Concerto in E flat (K. 271), Mozart's "Coronation" Concerto.* But: *the concerto.*

concertos (not *concerti*).

concluding. Use *ending* or *completing* unless the idea of a mental process is involved.

concrete. See **cement.**

conference (sports). Capitalize in names. *Western Conference.* But: *the conference.*

confidant (n.m.), **confidante** (n.f.).

confrère.

Congressional. Capitalize only when the reference is to the United States Congress.

Congressional committees and subcommittees. Capitalize committee names: *Ways and Means Commit-*

tee, Appropriations Committee. But: *the committee.* The word *subcommittee* is usually lower-case: *Ways and Means subcommittee, Appropriations subcommittee.* But capitalize if a subcommittee has a name of its own: *Senate Permanent Subcommittee on Investigations.*

Congressional Medal of Honor, the Medal of Honor, the medal.

Conn. for Connecticut after cities and towns.

-conscious. air-conscious, class-conscious, music-conscious.

consensus (not *consensus of opinion*).

conservative. Capitalize as noun or adjective only if the reference is to a political party or movement with *Conservative* in its name or to a member of such a group.

Consistory (Roman Catholic).

Constable John P. Manley, the constable.

Constitution. Capitalize when referring to the specific constitution of a nation or a state. But: *constitutional, unconstitutional.*

constitutional amendments. Capitalize amendments to the United States Constitution when referred to by number: *Fifth Amendment, 15th Amendment.* Also: *Income Tax Amendment.*

Consul (or **Consul General**) John P. Manley, Consul (or Consul General) Manley, the consul (or consul general).

contact. Do not use as a verb.

Continent. Capitalize after a name: African Continent, American Continent, European Continent, etc. Capitalize *the Continent* and *Continental* only when Europe is meant.

Continental Airlines.

contract bridge. Capitalize North, East, South, West. Lower-case spades, hearts, diamonds, clubs and no-trump, which is both singular and plural: *one no-trump, three no-trump.*

Also lower-case names of cards and spell them out when they appear singly: ace, king, queen, jack, ten, nine, eight, seven, six, five, four, three (never trey), two (or deuce). Use initials and numerals hyphenated, for two or more cards in combination: *He led into South's A-9* (not *ace-nine*). Use lower-case *x* as a symbol substituted for a numeral: *His holding in diamonds might have been K-x-x.*

Use numerals for all points except one in counting the value of a hand: *His hand was worth only 3 points. He had a 3-point hand. He had only one point.* Also use numerals for all match points or international match points except one. In scoring, use numerals for all points except fractions that are not combined with a whole number: *370 points, 379½ points, 2½ points, one-half point, half a point.*

In giving the distribution or division of a bridge hand or suit, always use numerals with hyphens: *He had a 5-3-3-2 hand. They hoped the suit would be divided 3-1.*

controlled.

Controller (not *Comptroller*) John P. Manley, the Controller (when referring to a governmental official).

controlling.

coolly.

co-op. But: *a cooperative.*

Copper Age.

copter (helicopter).

copy-. copybook, copycat. But: copy editor.

cord (vocal).

CORE for Congress of Racial Equality.

co-respondent.

Corn Belt.

cornerstone.

corporal. See **Cpl.**

corporations. See **company and corporation names.**

corps (military). Capitalize only when part of a name: *Artillery Corps, Signal Corps, Women's Army Corps, the corps.* For numbered corps use Roman numerals: *X Corps.*

corralled.

correspondent.

cortege.

Cortes (Spanish legislative body).

Cotton Belt.

Council of Foreign Ministers (NATO), the Council.

Council of the Organization of American States, the Council.

councilor (a member of a council).

counselor (one who gives counsel; the title of an embassy official).

counter-. counteralliance, counterargument, counterattack, counterbalance, countercharge, counterclaim, counterclockwise, counterirritant, counteroffensive, counterpart, counterplot, counterrevolution.

Countess Attlee, Lady Attlee, the Countess. In Britain, the title denotes the wife of an earl or the female equivalent of an earl; in other countries, the wife of a count or the female equivalent of a count. If the title is territorial: *the Countess of Derby, Lady Derby.*

country-. country-bred, countryman, countryside, countrywide.
But: country club.

county. Capitalize when part of a name: *Kings County, Ulster County.* But: *the county, the county government.*

County Clerk John P. Manley, the County Clerk.

coup d'état.

courts. Capitalize the names of courts: Appellate Division, County Court, Court of Appeals, Court of Claims, Court of Criminal Jurisdiction, International Court of Justice (the World Court), Supreme Court, Surrogate's Court, etc.

Second references to a court as such, but not to its judge or other presiding officer, are lower-cased; *the court.* There are two exceptions. It is *the Court* in such references to the Supreme Court of the United States and to the International Court of Justice. Also capitalize *Court* in direct references to the judge or other presiding officer of any court: *The Court ruled that the witness was out of order. The Court —The witness will proceed.*

The following and similar terms are to be lower-cased: administrator, appellant, coroner's jury, executor, grand jury, master, receiver, referee in bankruptcy.

In the Federal Court system, the appellate courts below the Supreme Court are the United States Courts of Appeals. These are circuit courts and should be referred to as *the United States Court of Appeals for the Fifth Circuit,* not *the Fifth Circuit Court of Appeals.* Below these courts are the United States District Courts. They may be referred to as *United States District Court* or *Federal District Court.*

See **Associate Justice, Chief Justice, Judge, Justice, Magistrate, Supreme Court, World Court.**

courthouse. Exception: United States *Court House* at Foley Square.

Courtlandt Avenue (Bronx).

court-martial, courts-martial.

Court of St. James's, St. James's Palace.

courtroom.

couturier is to be used for both men and women who are designers in haut couture. A couturière is a "little" dressmaker.

C.P.A. for certified public accountant.

Cpl. John P. Manley, Corporal Manley, the corporal.

crack-. crackbrained, crackpot, crack-up (n.).

crèche.

credit lines. Datelined stories by New York Times reporters that appear in the daily paper carry the following centered agate credit line above the dateline:

Special to The New York Times

News agency dispatches printed on Page 1 carry the following agate credit lines above the dateline:

By The Associated Press
By Reuters
By United Press International
Dispatch of The Times, London

Agency stories printed on inside pages carry the credits—(AP), (Reuters), (UPI), (Canadian Press)—in the dateline: DETROIT, Jan. 16 (AP)—etc. This style of credit also is used on Page 1 in matter that follows a 3-em dash.

crepe de chine.

crepe(s) suzette.

cricket. Runs are given in figures, but spell out the number of wickets under 10: *They scored 7 runs for two wickets.* There is a difference between a draw and a tie. A tied match, extremely rare, is one in which each team has the same score at the close of play. A draw is a match that has been abandoned or not completed to a decision. *Innings* is both singular and plural.

Criminal Courts Building.

crisis, crises.

crisscross.

criterion, criteria.

criticize.

cross-. cross-bill (law), cross-country, crosscurrent, cross-examination, cross-examine, cross-examiner, crossover, (n.), cross-purpose, cross-question (n., v.), crossroad, cross-town, crossway. But: cross reference, cross section.

Crossley (rating system).

crow's-nest (nautical).

crystallize.

Cubana Airlines.

Cunard Eagle Airways.

Cunard Line (Cunard Steam-Ship Company, Ltd.)

cupful, cupfuls.

cups (sports). Capitalize names of trophies: *America's Cup, Davis Cup.* See **America's Cup.**

cure-all.

curriculums.

Custom House.

cutoff (n.).

cutter. A single-masted yacht with two or more headsails. The mast is a little farther aft than in the sloop (which see). The distinction between cutter and sloop has almost disappeared. The word *cutter* is also used to designate a small Coast Guard vessel that is both powered and armed.

C. Z. for Canal Zone (Panama) after names of towns and cities.

Czar. Capitalize when referring to a former ruler of Russia. But: *baseball czar.*

Czechoslovak (person and adj.).

D

dachshund(s).

Dacron (trademark).

Dail Eireann.

Dalmatian (dog).

Dame Margot Fonteyn, Dame Margot. A dame who marries retains her title unless her husband holds a higher rank: *Dr. Roberto Arias and Dame Margot Fonteyn de Arias.*

dance. Capitalize in a title: *Schubert's German Dances,* "*Dance of the Hours,*" "*Danse Macabre.*" Also: *a Chopin waltz, Chopin's Waltz in A flat.* Similarly treat *bourree, gavotte, gigue, hornpipe, minuet* and *sarabande.*

Dandie Dinmont terrier.

D.A.R. for Daughters of the American Revolution.

Dardanelles. It is *the Dardanelles,* not *Dardanelles Strait.*

dark-. dark-eyed, dark-haired, darkroom (photography).

Dark Ages.

dash. The dash is often misused for the comma: *John—who was badly hurt last year—was pronounced fit today. His friends—Mr. and Mrs. Jones—were late.* But the dash is properly used when what follows is a series punctuated by commas: *The Administration will face many problems — unemployment, school segregation, declining revenue and rising Government costs—during the present session of Congress.* Here the dash also is needed to avoid confusion: *The costs—taxes and lawyers' fees—were higher than he had expected.*

Another use of the dash is to mark an abrupt change in continuity of expression: "*The balance of payments is—but you know all that.*" Interruptions in dialogue and Q. and A. matter can also be marked by the dash. It may also precede *namely, viz., i.e.* and similar words and abbreviations.

Do not use a dash together with a comma, semicolon or colon.

In datelines the dash is used after the date: SCRANTON, Pa., Nov. 12—etc.

data (pl.), **datum** (sing., but rare).

datelines. Cities and towns are set all caps, with the country or state in upper and lower case:

LAGOS, Nigeria, March 22—

SUGAR HILL, N.H., July 16 (AP)—

CHARLOTTE, N. C., Friday, Sept. 18 (AP)—

In shipboard datelines, include a locating phrase:

ABOARD U.S.S. SARATOGA, Guantanamo Bay, Cuba, July 16—

The Soviet Union is the only foreign country whose name is abbreviated (U.S.S.R.) in a dateline. The abbreviations of states of the United States and Canadian provinces and some other abbreviations that are to be used in datelines are listed separately and alphabetically. When the names of the city and the country are identical, as in the cases of Guatemala and Panama, use only one.

Some major United States and foreign cities and some widely known smaller cities in the United States do not require the identifying state or country in the dateline. Here is a list of such cities:

United States

ALBANY	BALTIMORE
ANCHORAGE	BATON ROUGE
ATLANTA	BOSTON
ATLANTIC CITY	BUFFALO

CHATTANOOGA
CHICAGO
CINCINNATI
CLEVELAND
COLORADO
  SPRINGS
DALLAS
DENVER
DETROIT
EL PASO
FORT WORTH
HARTFORD
HOLLYWOOD
HONOLULU
HOUSTON
INDIANAPOLIS
IOWA CITY
JERSEY CITY
LOS ANGELES
MEMPHIS
MIAMI
MILWAUKEE
MINNEAPOLIS
NASHVILLE

NEWARK
NEW HAVEN
NEW ORLEANS
OKLAHOMA
  CITY
OMAHA
PHILADELPHIA
PITTSBURGH
RENO
RICHMOND
ROCHESTER
SALT LAKE
  CITY
SAN DIEGO
SAN FRANCISCO
SEATTLE
ST. LOUIS
ST. PAUL
SYRACUSE
TRENTON
WASHINGTON
WHITE PLAINS
YONKERS

Foreign

ATHENS
BERLIN
BERNE
BONN
BRUSSELS
BUCHAREST
BUDAPEST
BUENOS AIRES
CAIRO
CAPETOWN
DUBLIN
GENEVA
GUATEMALA
HAVANA
HONG KONG
LENINGRAD
LISBON
LONDON
LUXEMBOURG
MADRID
MANILA

MEXICO CITY
MONTREAL
MOSCOW
NANKING
NEW DELHI
OTTAWA
PANAMA
PARIS
PEKING
PRAGUE
RIO DE JANEIRO
ROME
SAN SALVADOR
SHANGHAI
SINGAPORE
STOCKHOLM
TEL AVIV
TOKYO
TORONTO
VIENNA
WARSAW

Shoulder dates are indented one em from the right, with the city in caps and small caps, and with or without the credit line, depending on the style for the section of the paper in which the story appears.

Thus:

By JOHN P. MANLEY

Special to The New York Times

LAGOS, Nigeria.

dates. See **days, weeks, months, years, decades, centuries.**

daylight time. Do not capitalize: *9 A.M. Eastern daylight time.* Abbreviation: *E.D.T.*

days. Numerals are used for days of the month when they follow the month: *April 1, 1961.* This form should be used only in quoted matter: *6th of January.*

D.D. for Doctor of Divinity.

D.D.S. for Doctor of Dental Surgery.

DDT (insecticide).

death-. deathbed, death's-head, deathtrap, deathwatch. But: death knell, death rate.

debacle.

debris.

debut.

debutante.

Dec. for December before numerals: *Dec. 17.*

decades of years may be spelled out (the preferred form in stories) or given in figures: *the nineteen-sixties, the 1960's.* When the century is omitted in stories, the decade is spelled out and lower-cased: *the sixties.* In headlines, *60's* may be used. Capitalize special designations like *the Roaring Twenties.* See **years.**

decimals. Use figures for all numbers that contain decimals: *3.4 inches of rain, 22.25 inches of snow.* If the figure is entirely a decimal, use a cipher before the point: *0.3.* See **fractions.**

décolletage (n.), **décolleté** (adj.).

décor.

Decoration Day (Memorial Day).

deductible.

deep-, -deep. deep-rooted, deep-sea (adj.), deep-seated, deepwater (adj.).
Also: ankle-deep, waist-deep.

Deepfreeze is a trademark name for a food freezer. In general references to this type of equipment, *food freezer, home freezer* or *freezer* should be used. Something shelved or put off indefinitely may be said to be in the *deep freeze.*

Deep South.

deerhound.

defensible.

degrees. See **academic degrees and titles, temperature.**

Deity. Capitalize all appellations such as *Holy Ghost, Son of Man, Supreme Being,* and personal pronouns such as *His, Him, Thee, Thou,* but not the relative pronouns *who, whom,* etc.

déjeuner.

Del. for Delaware after cities and towns.

Delaware & Hudson Railroad.

delegate at large. No hyphens.

Delta Air Lines.

Delta Line (Mississippi Shipping Company, Inc.).

demagogy.

démarche.

demi-. demi-Christian, demigod, demimonde, demitasse.

Democratic National Convention, the national convention, the convention.

Democratic party.

démodé.

denouement.

Denver & Rio Grande Western Railroad, the Rio Grande.

department. Capitalize when part of the name of an agency of government: *Health Department, Conservation Department, State Department.* Do not capitalize academic departments: *department of English, department of political science.* The abbreviation (*Dept.*) may be used in agate and other special matter, but not in stories or headlines.

Depression (of the nineteen-thirties).

deputy. Capitalize when part of a title preceding a name: *Deputy Sheriff John P. Manley.* Do not capitalize in second references unless the position so titled is a major one: the *Deputy Attorney General, the Deputy Mayor* (of New York), *the Deputy Premier, the Deputy United States Representative, etc.* But: *the deputy sheriff.* Capitalize all specific references to members of foreign parliaments so designated. See **assistant.**

de rigueur.

desiccate.

Detroit Stock Exchange.

Detroit, Toledo & Ironton Railroad.

Deutsche mark.

Devil. Capitalize if Satan is meant, but lower-case *devils* and *a devil.*

devotee.

DEW for distant early warning, as in *DEW line.*

Dexedrine (trademark).

diarrhea.

Diaspora.

Dictaphone (trademark).

dictionaries. Do not quote their titles; capitalize principal words.

die-hard.

diesel.

Diet (legislative body). Capitalize all specific references.

dietitian.

dilettante(s).

dimensions, measurement and proportion. They are usually given in figures: *2 by 4, 7 feet 3 inches by 10 feet 5 inches* (no commas), *5 feet 10 inches tall, 6 years 5 months 13 days* (age), *5 parts gin 1 part vermouth, 2 to 1, 50-50, odds of 4 to 3, 8-to-1 shot.* Also: *2½ by 4, 3¼ inches long, 15½-foot boat.*

diphtheria.

disk.

district. Capitalize when part of a name: *Second Election District, 10th Assembly District, 17th Congressional District, District of Columbia, etc.* The abbreviation (*Dist.*) may be used in agate and other special matter, but not in stories or headlines. *District* standing alone is capitalized only when the District of Columbia is meant.

division (military). Spell out numerical designations through the ninth

and then use figures: *Fifth Division, 34th Division; the division.*

Dniepropetrovsk (U.S.S.R.).

Dnieprostroy (U.S.S.R.).

Dobbs Ferry (N.Y.).

Doberman pinscher.

dock (n.). It is not a pier or wharf, but the water between piers or wharves.

dock-. dockmaster, dockside, dockyard. But: dock hand.

dog-days.

dogs and dog shows. The breeds are listed separately and alphabetically. The dog singled out for top honors in an all-breed show is named best in show or gains the best-in-show award, but does not *win* the show.

dollars and cents. Sums of dollars and cents are usually set in figures: *25 cents, $10, $12.25, $10,000, $1,000,000.* Round-number and indefinite amounts may also be spelled out: *half a million, a quarter of a million, a million and a half dollars, million-dollar suit, twenty-five billion dollars, a million or more, ten or eleven thousand dollars, one dollar.* Large round numbers sometimes are set as follows: *$200 million, $3.5 million* (for $3,500,000), *$16 billion.* But use of this form in headlines is discouraged. Since *$100 Billion Budget* is one unit longer than *100-Billion Budget* the latter tends to be used more, but the use of both forms would be inconsistent. Therefore the *100-Billion* form is favored when there are reasons for not using the dollar sign with the sum entirely in figures. In sums involving only cents, spell out *cents* or *cent* in ordinary matter: *26 cents a dozen, 1-cent tax, 4-cent stamp, 9 cents apiece.* But: *They couldn't find one* (not *1*) *red cent.* In headlines, financial quotations and tabular matter, the symbol may be used: 3C, 26C.

door-. doorbell, doorknob, doorman, doorstep. But: door key.

Douay Version (of the Bible; Roman Catholic).

double-. double-barreled, double-breasted, double-cross (n., v.), double-dyed, double-header, double-quick.

Dowager Marchioness of Bute, the; Lady Bute, the Marchioness. A dowager peeress in Britain is the earliest surviving widow of a previous holder of the title. Succeeding widows use their given name before the title: *Alice Marchioness of Bute, Lady Bute, the Marchioness.*

down-. downcast, downhearted, downhill, downstairs, downtown, downtrodden.

Down East.

Dr. John P. Manley, Dr. Manley, the doctor.

draft. Use instead of *draught* for a current of air. Also: *draft beer, draftsman.*

drop-kick (n., v., adj.), **drop-kicking.**

drought.

drug. Do not use as a synonym for *narcotic.*

drydock.

Duchess of Bedford, the; the Duchess.

due to. *Due* is an adjective and must have a noun to modify: *His fall was due to the icy sidewalk.* Not: *He fell due to the icy sidewalk.*

dueling, duelist.

Duke of Bedford, the; the Duke.

Duluth, Missabe & Iron Range Railway.

dumfounded.

DuMont (television).

Dupont Circle (Washington).

du Pont de Nemours & Co.

Düsseldorf.

Dutch. Dutch elm disease, Dutch oven, Dutch treat, Dutch uncle.

Dutchess County.

Dynel (trademark).

E

each other, one another. Two persons look at *each other;* more than two look at *one another.*

Earl Attlee, Lord Attlee, the Earl.

Earl of Derby, the; Lord Derby, the Earl.

earth satellites. Do not quote their names: *Discoverer XX, Explorer VI, Sputnik III.* Do not capitalize *a sputnik, the sputnik.*

East, east. Capitalize when referring to that geographic region of the United States and to the Communist side in the ideological division of the world. Lower-case as a point of the compass.

Eastchester, N. Y.; East Chester, N. Y. Eastchester is in Westchester County, East Chester in Orange.

East Coast, east coast. Capitalize when referring to the region of the United States lying along the shoreline of the Atlantic Ocean; lower-case when referring to the actual shoreline. Use *the Coast* for the West Coast only.

East End (London).

Eastern Air Lines.

Eastern, eastern. Capitalize when referring to the East (geographic region) of the United States and to the Communist side in the ideological division of the world. But: *eastern New York, eastern France, eastern half, etc.*

Easterner. Capitalize when referring to persons who were born in or are inhabitants of the East (United States).

East Hampton (L.I.).

Eastern Seaboard. The region of the United States lying along the Atlantic coast. Also *the Atlantic Seaboard.*

Eastern Shore (region on Chesapeake Bay).

Eastern standard (or **daylight**) **time** (E.S.T., E.D.T.).

East Side. Capitalize when regularly used to designate a section of a city.

easy-going.

éclat.

ecstasy.

El Al Israel Airlines.

élan.

-elect. president-elect, vice president-elect, governor-elect, *etc.* Capitalize before names (title only) and when standing alone if the office is gov-ernmental and the reference specific: *Senator-elect John P. Manley, the Senator-elect.*

Election Day.

election districts. See **district.**

Electoral College.

electrical, electronic. The words should not be used interchangeably. An ordinary light bulb or a motor is electrical. A radio receiver, a TV set or a modern computer is electronic, which means that the flow of electrons through it is controlled by vacuum tubes, transistors or other solid-state devices.

élite.

ellipsis should be indicated only in important documents, not in ordinary textual matter. Use three points (not asterisks) to indicate an omission in the middle of a sentence and four points for an omission at the end of a sentence. To indicate the omission of entire paragraphs use a centered line of three points between paragraphs: .   .   .

Embankment (London).

embarrassment.

embassy. Lower-case when standing alone. But: *the United States Embassy, the French Embassy.*

emeritus. It should be *Dr. John P. Manley, professor emeritus* (or *emeritus professor) of political science,* not *professor of political science emeritus.*

émigré.

Emperor Haile Selassie, the Emperor.

employe(s).

empty-handed.

enclose.

enclosure.

encyclopedias. Do not quote their titles; capitalize principal words.

ended, ending. Use *ended* for the past, *ending* for the future: *the period ended* (last) *Jan. 15, the period ending* (next) *June 15.*

endorse.

enforce.

English setter.

English springer spaniel.

enroll.

enrollment.

Ens. John P. Manley, Ensign Manley, the ensign.

entr'acte.

entree.

entrepôt.

entrust.

envelop (v.), **envelope** (n.).

épée.

equaled, equaling.

equally as. Do not use the words together; one suffices.

Equator. But lower-case *equatorial.*

eras. See **ages and eras of history.**

Erie-Lackawanna Railroad.

Eskimo, Eskimos.

esthetic.

et cetera. Use *etc.* as the abbreviation.

Eton collar, Eton jacket.

étude.

Euratom for European Atomic Energy Community.

European Economic Community (Common Market, which see).

European Free Trade Association (Outer Seven, which see).

European Payments Union, the union.

Evangelical United Brethren Church.

ever-. ever-faithful, evergreen, ever-lasting, evermore, ever-present, ever-ready.

every-. everybody, everyday (adj.), everyone, everything, everywhere.

evildoer.

ex-. The hyphen is used in this form: *ex-champion, ex-President, ex-tennis champion.* In stories, the adjective *former* is generally preferred, but *ex-*, of course, is almost always used in headlines. Do not hyphenate *ex officio,* even when in adjectival form (*ex officio chairman*), or such expressions as *ex cathedra, ex dividend, ex parte, ex post facto.*

exclamation mark. It is rarely needed in news stories, except in quoted matter: *"To the gallows!" the crowd shouted. "That is a lie!" he roared.*

executive branch (of the United States Government). Also: *legislative branch.*

Executive Mansion.

Executive order (by a President of the United States). But capitalize *Order* if it is numbered: *Executive Order 39.*

exhilarate.

Export-Import Bank, the bank.

exposé (n.).

extra-. extra-artistic, extracurricular, extra-fine, extrajudical, extraordinary, extraterritorial.

eyewitness.

F

F.A.A. for Federal Aviation Agency.

facade.

fact-finding (adj.).

fade-. fadeaway (n.), fadeout (n.).

fall (autumn).

fallout (n.).

Fanny May for Federal National Mortgage Association. Its bonds are known as Fanny Mays.

fantasy (music). In titles in which the word appears without quotation marks, use the English spelling: *Schubert's Fantasy* (not *Fantasia*) *in C for Violin and Piano (Op. 159).*

F.A.O. for Food and Agriculture Organization.

far-. far-fetched, far-flung, far-reaching, far-seeing.

Far East. It comprises China, Japan, North Korea, South Korea, the Philippines, the Pacific littoral of the Soviet Union (the Soviet Far East) and various Pacific islands.

farm-. farmhand, farmhouse, farmyard.

Far North.

Far West (of the United States).

Farrell Lines.

farther, further. Use *farther* for distance, *further* for continuation.

Fascism. Capitalize in reference to an organized Fascist party or movement.

Fascist, Fascists. Capitalize as nouns designating members of an organized Fascist party or movement. Capitalize *Fascist* as an adjective in a similar sense. But: *The Senator said his rival was a fascist* (or *had fascist tendencies*).

Father (clerical title) may be used in second references to Roman Catholic priests and to some Protestant Episcopal clergymen: *the Rev. John P. Manley, Father Manley.*

Father's Day.

faultfinder.

faux pas.

F.C.C. for Federal Communications Commission.

feast days. See holidays.

featherweight (n., adj.).

feature. Avoid as a verb.

Feb. for February before numerals: *Feb. 12.*

Federal. Capitalize when part of a name or when used as an adjective synonymous with United States: *Federal Reserve Board, Federal troops, Federal courts.* Lower-case when used in a general sense: *the federal principle of government.* Also: *federally.*

Federal Building.

Federal courts. See courts.

fellow. Do not use the hyphen in this form: *fellow American, fellow citizen, fellow worker.*

fellow (academic). *He is the John P. Manley Fellow. He is a fellow at the university.* Capitalize the formal title of a fellowship: *the John P. Manley Fellowship in History.*

ferryboat.

ferule (ruler), **ferrule** (metal cap).

fete.

F.H.A. for Federal Housing Administration.

fiancé, fiancée.

Fiberglas (trademark).

Field Marshal Viscount Montgomery of Alamein, Viscount Montgomery, Lord Montgomery, Field Marshal Montgomery. It is never *Marshal* Montgomery.

fifth column.

figures. See **numbers.**

films. Quote their titles; capitalize principal words.

filmstrip.

fire-. firearms, firebug, fire-escape, fireproof, firetrap.

fire (v.). Do not use to mean dismissal from a job.

Fire Department.

First Lieut. John P. Manley, Lieutenant Manley, the lieutenant.

First Sgt. John P. Manley, Sergeant Manley, the sergeant.

Fishers Island.

Five Years Meeting of Friends (Quakers).

Fla. for Florida after cities and towns.

flag-. flagpole, flagstaff.

flat-coated retriever.

fleet. Capitalize only when part of a title: *Atlantic Fleet, British Grand Fleet.*

fleur de lis.

flier (an airman), **flyer** (a crack train).

Flight Lieut. (British) John P. Manley, Flight Lieutenant Manley, the flight lieutenant.

floor leader. Capitalize only when it appears before a name: *Floor Leader John P. Manley. He is the floor leader.*

Florida East Coast Railway.

Flushing Meadow.

Flying Tiger Line.

f.o.b. for free on board.

focused.

-fold. twofold, threefold, manifold, manyfold.

folk(-). folk dance (n.), folk-dance (adj.), folklore, folk music, folk singers, folk song.

follow-. follow-through (n.), follow-up (n.).

fool-. foolhardy, foolproof, foolscap.

foot-. foothill, footloose, footman, footpad, footpath, foot-pound, footprint, footstep, footwear. But: foot race.

football. Points and scores are given in figures: *He scored 9 points in the* second quarter. *Columbia won, 13 to 6.* Yards are also given in figures: *He gained 3 yards. He passed 21 yards to the 8-yard line.* Spell out numbers of touchdowns and downs below 10. *He scored two touchdowns, making a total of 13 for the season. It was a first down.*

Do not capitalize the *all* in *all-America* (no *n*) *player, all-America team, all-East tackle*, etc. But: *He was an all-American at Yale.*

Avoid *fracas, fray, grid, gridder, win* (as a noun), *pigskin* and similar worn-out terms.

forbear (avoid, shun), **forebear** (ancestor).

fore-. forefather, forefront, foreknowledge, foremast, forestall, foretaste, foretopmast, foretopsail, forewarn.

Foreign Legion, the legion.

Foreign Minister (or Secretary) John P. Manley, the Foreign Minister or Foreign Secretary.

Foreign Service (of the United States).

foreign words. See **accent marks.**

forgo (to refrain from).

former. In stories *former,* as in *former President,* is generally preferred to *ex-,* but *ex-* is, of course, almost always used in headlines.

Formica (trademark).

forswear.

fort. Spell out and capitalize in ordinary reading matter when part of a name: *Fort Hamilton.* The abbreviation (*Ft.*) may be used with the name in headlines and in agate and other special matter.

Fort Du Pont.

Fourth of July.

fowl. (Sing. and pl.).

foxhound.

F.P.C. for Federal Power Commission.

fractions. Spell out in ordinary matter when the fraction appears by itself: *a quarter of an inch, three-quarters of an inch, half a gallon, one-half gallon, two-tenths, one-fortieth, ten-hundredths* (not *ten one-hundredths*), *twenty-one thirty-seconds, sixty-three thousandths.* Use numerals whenever the fraction appears with a full number in ages, dimensions, measures, etc.: *3½-year-old, 3½ by 2½* (or *3.5 by 2.5*), *5½-pound chicken.* In other cases, follow the rule for spelling out up to 10: *He reigned for six and one-half* (or *a half*) *years. His reign lasted 31½ years.* See **decimals.**

frame-up (n.).

François.

francs and centimes. Spell out when the figures are given: *5 francs, 15,000,000 francs, 15 centimes.*

Frankfurt (Germany).

fraternal societies. Capitalize their names: *Knights of Columbus, Masons, Odd Fellows,* etc. Also capitalize the titles of their officers: *Grand Ruler, Exalted Ruler, Sachem,* etc.

Fraunces Tavern.

freelance.

French bulldog.

french cuff.

french door.

french-fried potatoes.

French Line (Compagnie Générale Transatlantique).

frère.

freshman (class and member of that class).

Frigidaire (trademark).

F.T.C. for Federal Trade Commission.

Führer.

fulfill.

fullback.

Fundamentalist (religious designation).

Furness Bermuda Line.

furor.

further. See **farther, further.**

fusillade.

G

Ga. for Georgia after cities and towns.

gaiety, gaily.

gale. Do not use unless the wind meets the Weather Bureau's specifications for a gale—25 to 75 miles an hour.

gamut. You can run a *gamut* (a scale of notes) or a *gantlet* (a flogging ordeal) literally or figuratively.

gamy.

gangway.

gantlet is a flogging ordeal.

garçon.

gas. When used to mean gasoline, quote it only if the context does not make clear that gasoline is meant.

gauge.

gauntlet is a glove, not a flogging ordeal.

GATT for General Agreement on Tariffs and Trade.

gazetteers. Do not quote their titles; capitalize principal words.

gefilte fish.

Gen. John P. Manley, General Manley, the general.

General Assembly (United Nations), the Assembly.

Generalissimo John P. Manley, the generalissimo.

General of the Army John P. Manley, General Manley, the general.

General Staff. The German General Staff, the General Staff, a general staff.

genoa (sail), **genoese jib.**

genus and species. Capitalize the name of a phylum, class, order, family or genus. Do not capitalize the name of a species. *The violet belongs to the genus Viola. The tiger (Felis tigris) is carnivorous.*

geographic names. The authority for the spelling of geographic names is the Columbia Lippincott Gazetteer of the World. For easy reference, some place names are listed in the Style Book separately and alphabetically.

Georgia & Florida Railroad.

Germanys. This, not German*ies*, is the proper plural for Germany. See **plurals of proper names.**

getaway (n.).

Ghanaian (person and adj.).

G.I. for general issue, Government issue and soldiers (pl. *G.I.'s*). A marine or a Navy man is not a G.I.

G.I. bill of rights.

gibe (taunt).

Gibraltar, Strait of.

gilt-edge.

Gimbels. This form (no apostrophe) may be used in references to the New York store. When *Gimbel Brothers* is used, always spell out *Brothers*. The parent company is *Gimbel Brothers, Inc.*

Girl Scout, a Scout, the Scouts.

give-away (n.).

gladiolus, gladioluses.

glamour, glamorous.

Glens Falls (N.Y.).

G.N.P. for gross national product.

goalkeeper.

go-between.

God (the Supreme Being).

god-. godfather, godless, godlike, godmother, godsend, godson, godspeed.

golden retriever.

golf. Spell out the number of holes, tees and strokes below 10: *He took six strokes on the ninth hole. He fell behind on the 10th hole.* But: *He shot a 6.* Also: *72-hole tournament, 2-foot putt, 95 yards.* The totals of in and out play are set thus: 36, 36—72. Handicap totals: 83—10—73.

Competition is held at medal play (lowest score wins) and match play (direct elimination). Some tournaments combine both, with qualifying medal play preceding match play.

Do not capitalize *open* and *amateur* in names of tournaments, except the United States (or National) Open, United States Amateur, British Open and British Amateur.

Do not use *birdie, bogey* and *par* as verbs.

good-by.

good day (greeting or farewell).

Good Friday.

good morning (greeting or farewell).

good night (farewell).

goodwill.

gothic.

Götterdämmerung.

Gov. John P. Manley (of a state), Governor Manley, the Governor.

Government, government. Capitalize when referring to specific national government: *the United States Government, the Pakistani Government.* Also capitalize in other references, singular and plural, to specific national governments and, in some countries like those of the British Commonwealth, to the party in power: *The Government acted. The NATO Governments replied.* Also capitalize the adjective form in reference to specific national governments: *Government bonds, Government bureaus.* Lower-case state, provincial and municipal governments: *the city government, etc.* Also lower-case when used in a general sense: *the principles of government.*

governmental. Lower-case unless it is part of a name.

Governor-elect John P. Manley, Governor-elect Manley, the Governor-elect (of a state).

governorship.

Governors Island.

Grace Line.

Grand Central Terminal.

grandstand.

grave accent. See **accent marks.**

gray. But: *greyhound.*

great-. great-grandchild, great-granddaughter, great-grandfather, great-grandmother, great-grandson.

Great Dane.

Great Lakes, the lakes.

Great Northern Railway.

Greek Archdiocese of North and South America.

Greek Line.

Greenwich mean time (G.M.T.).

greyhound.

grippe.

Group Capt. (British) John P. Manley, Group Captain Manley, the group captain.

grownup (n.), **grown-up** (adj.).

grueling.

gruesome.

Guadalupe (Mexico).

Guadeloupe (W.I.).

guarantee (not *guaranty*).

gubernatorial. But *governership* is preferred.

guerrilla.

guidebook.

Gulf Coast, gulf coast. Capitalize when referring to the region of the United States lying along the Gulf of Mexico; lower-case when referring to the actual shoreline. Capitalize *Gulf Coast States.*

Gulf, Mobile & Ohio Railroad.

Gulf Stream. But: *Gulfstream Park.*

gun-. gunfire, gunman, gunpowder, gunshot, gunsmith, gun-shy.

Gunnery Sgt. John P. Manley, Sergeant Manley, the sergeant.

gypsy.

H

habitué.

Habsburg (not *Hapsburg*).

Hades. But lower-case *hell.*

Hague, The.

hair-. hairbreadth, haircut, hairdresser, hairdressing, hairtrigger. But: hair shirt. Also: red-haired (not red-*headed*).

Haiti, Haitian.

Haitien (Cape).

half-. half-afraid, half-and-half (the drink), halfback, half-brother, half-clad, half-done, half-dozen (adj.), half-full, halfhearted, half-holiday, half-jokingly, halfpenny, halftone, halfway. But: half dollar, half pay.

half-mast, half-staff. Flags on ships and at naval installations ashore are flown at *half-mast;* flags elsewhere ashore are flown at *half-staff.*

hall-. hallboy, hallmark, hallway.

Halloween.

halo, halos.

Hamburg-American Line.

hammer throw.

hand-. handball, handbag, handbill, handbook, handful(s), handmade, handout (n.), handshake, handspring.

handyman (odd-jobs man).

hangar (shed).

hanged (executed).

hanger(s)-on.

hangover (n.).

Hanukkah (Feast of Lights).

hara-kiri.

harass.

hard-. hard-bitten, hard-boiled, hard-earned, hardhearted, hardwood.

harebrained.

Harts Island.

harum-scarum.

hatrack.

Hawaii, Hawaiian. Do not abbreviate Hawaii after cities and towns.

hay-. hayfield, haymaker, hayrick, haystack. But: hay fever.

H-bomb. It may be used in stories as well as headlines, but in stories *hydrogen bomb* is preferred unless the context seems to call for *H-bomb*. In upper-and-lower-case headlines, the *b* is capitalized: *H-Bomb.*

head-. headdress, headhunter, headman, headmaster (which see),

headmistress, head-on, headroom, headstart, headstrong, headway, headwind.

headline capitalization. See **capitalization.**

Headmaster John P. Manley, the headmaster.

headquarters (military). *First Army Headquarters, the headquarters.*

heart condition. Do not use unless the condition is described. Every heart has some kind of condition. Say *heart ailment, disease, injury, etc.*

heart-. -hearted. heartbreak, heartbroken, heartfelt. Also: halfhearted, lionhearted, softhearted.

heaven. Lower-case except in this sense: *I thank Heaven.*

heavyweight (n. and adj., boxing).

Heights (Brooklyn). Also: *the Heights.*

hell. But capitalize *Hades.*

helter-skelter.

Hepplewhite (furniture).

herculean.

here-. hereabout, hereafter, herein, hereinafter, hereto.

Hialeah Race Course. But it is *a racecourse.*

Hias may be used, without the article, in second references to the United Hias Service.

hide-. hide-and-seek (n.), hideaway (n.), hidebound, hide-out (n.).

high-. highball (drink), highbrow (n. and adj.), high-grade (adj.),

highhanded, highlight (n. and v.),
high-power (adj.), highroad,
highway, highwayman.

High Holy Days (Jewish).

high mass. It is sung, not said. See
mass.

hijack may be used to mean the steal·
ing or other illegal seizure of a con-
veyance—land, air or sea—or its con-
tents while in transit. The word,
which originally meant to rob boot-
leggers or rum-runners, did not die
with Prohibition. *Hijacking* is the
noun.

hike. Do not use as a synonym for increase, either noun or verb.

hill-. hillbilly, hillside, hilltop.

hippopotamus, hippopotamuses.

His Holiness (the Pope). Use only in
quoted matter.

His Majesty, Her Majesty and similar designations are to be used only
in quoted matter.

Hispaniola (island comprising Do-
minican Republic and Haiti).

hit-. hit-and-miss, hit-and-run,
hit-run (in headlines).

hitchhike (v.), **hitchhiker.**

hockey. Scores are given in figures:
The Rangers won, 3 to 0. Numbers of
goals below 10 and of periods are
spelled out: *He scored three goals in
the second period.* But: *The score at
the end of the second period was 3
to 1.*

hocus-pocus.

Ho-Ho-Kus (N. J.).

holdup. The *holdup* man *holds up* the
victim of the *holdup.*

hole-in-one (n. and adj.).

holidays are listed separately and
alphabetically.

Holland-America Line.

holy communion.

Holy Father (the Pope). Use only in
quoted matter.

Holy See. The Roman see of the Roman Catholic Church.

Holy Week (the week before Easter).

home-. homemade, homemaker,
homeowner, homespun,
homestretch, homework. But:
home plate, home rule, home run.

Home Lines.

Hon., for Honorable before a name,
is not to be used, except in quoted
matter.

Hong Kong.

Hoosac Tunnel.

Hoosick Falls.

horror-struck.

hors de combat.

horse(-). horseplay, horsepower,
horse race, horse racing.

horse races. Capitalize *Kentucky
Derby, Belmont Stakes, One Thousand Guineas, Suburban Handicap,
etc.*

horse racing. Use figures for times
of races: *2:39.* The fraction is used
rather than the decimal: *1:12⅘.*
Spell out lengths under 10 unless
they contain a fraction: *three
lengths, 3½ lengths, 12 lengths.*

The first time prices are mentioned in a story, the type of bet

should be specified. *He paid $4.60 for $2 to win. He returned $18.40, $9.60 and $5.40 for $2 across the board.* Exact odds should be used. If the odds are 35 cents to the dollar, the horse is 7 to 20 (or 7—20) rather than 1 to 3. If the payoff is $4.10 for $2, the odds are 21 to 20, not even money. Exception: If the price is comparatively high, the odds may be rounded out. Thus a horse paying $38.20 for $2 may be listed as 18 to 1 rather than 181—10.

Thoroughbred horses run in stakes (sing. and pl.), harness horses in a stake (sing.) or stakes (pl.).

Harness races are trotted or paced, not run. The words *break* and *broke* should be used with care in harness stories. *He broke from the No. 4 post* could mean either that the horse started from that post or that he broke his stride.

If the horse's name is used in the story, the horse is referred to as *he* or *she*, not *it*. Gelded horses are refered to as *he*. Roman, not Arabic numerals, are used in horses' names: *Icare IV, Shannon II, etc.*

hot-blooded.

hotels. Capitalize their names: *Waldorf-Astoria Hotel.* Generally, but not always, *Hotel* follows the name.

hours. See **time.**

house-. houseboat, houseboy, housebroken, housekeeper, housemaid, housetop, housewife, housework.

House of Commons, the Commons.

House of Lords, the Lords.

House of Representatives (United States), the House.

houses and estates. Do not quote their names: *Blair House, The Elms.*

hove-to.

Hudson & Manhattan Railroad Company, the H. & M., the Hudson Tubes.

Hungarian Reformed Church in America.

hurly-burly.

hurricanes. Do not personalize by overuse of the names (*Alice, Betsy, etc.*) assigned to them. *Hurricane Alice struck the city* is all right, but *Alice behaved capriciously* is not. Do not call a storm a hurricane unless it meets the Weather Bureau specifications. One of them is wind above 75 miles an hour.

hymns. Quote their titles; capitalize principal words.

hyphen. Many compounds are formed with the hyphen as a connector, but as such words become established the hyphen is often dropped in favor of the solid form. (Compounds are listed separately and alphabetically.)

The hyphen is used in constructions like these: *three-mile hike, 30-car train.* It also is used to avoid confusion in words like *re-form* (meaning to form again).

Hyphens should not be used in constructions like the following if the meaning is clear without them: *Sales Tax Bill, foreign aid plan.* But: *Pay-as-You-Go Bill.* The hyphen is not needed in these forms: *navy blue skirt, dark green paint.*

In many compounds, the hyphen should be used to avoid ambiguity or absurdity: *small-business man,* not *small businessman* (note separation of solid compound; see **com-**

pound words); *unfair-practices charge,* not *unfair practices charge.*

Chiefly because of the typographical hazard, it is best to avoid suspensive hyphens, which are hyphens used thus: *On successive days there were three-, five- and nine-inch snowfalls.* Make it *three-inch, five-inch and nine-inch.*

Do not use the hyphen to connect an adverb ending in *ly* with a participle in such phrases as *newly married couple, elegantly furnished house.*

Street numbers in Queens take the hyphen: *107-71 111th Street.*

I

Iberia Air Lines of Spain.

I.C.A. for International Cooperation Administration.

ICBM for intercontinental ballistic missile.

I.C.C. for Interstate Commerce Commission.

ice(-). iceberg, iceboat, icebound, icecap, ice cream, ice floe, iceman, ice pack, ice water.

ice age.

Icelandic Airlines.

Illinois Central Railroad.

includes. Do not use if what follows is a complete listing.

Incres Line.

Idaho. Do not abbreviate after cities and towns.

idée fixe.

Idlewild Airport may be used instead of the official name, New York International Airport. The single word *Idlewild* will suffice for second references in stories and first references in headlines.

I.L.A. for International Longshoremen's Association.

I.L.G.W.U. for International Ladies Garment Workers Union.

ill-. ill-advised, ill-defined, ill-fated, ill-humored, ill-mannered, ill-natured, ill-omened, ill-tempered, ill-timed, ill-treated. But: ill humor, ill will.

Ill. for Illinois after cities and towns.

I.L.O. for International Labor Organization.

impanel.

impasse.

imply, infer. A speaker implies; a listener infers.

impostor.

in-. inbound, indoor, infield, infighting, in-law.

in, into. These words are often misused, especially in headlines. You jump *into* the lake. You swim *in* it.

inasmuch as.

Inauguration Day.

incommunicado.

IND for Independent Subway System.

Ind. for Indiana after cities and towns.

indispensable.

Indochina. Former French Indochina comprised the now independent states of Cambodia, Laos, North Vietnam and South Vietnam.

Indonesian names. Many Indonesians, like Sukarno, have only one name. First references to persons with titles, of course, present no problems: *President Sukarno.* But if he had no title, it would be *Mr. Sukarno* in first references.

infrared.

ingénue.

inimitable.

innocuous.

innuendo.

inoculate.

inquire.

insigne (sing.), **insignia** (pl.).

insofar as.

insomuch as.

Inspector John P. Manley, the inspector.

install, installment.

instill, instilling.

insure.

inter-. interallied, intercollegiate, interracial, interstate.

intern (confine), **interne** (doctor).

International Brotherhood of Teamsters may be used in first references instead of the full name, the International Brotherhood of Teamsters, Chauffeurs, Warehousemen and Helpers. Also: *the teamsters, the teamsters' union.*

International Convention of Christian Churches (Disciples of Christ).

International Monetary Fund, the fund.

interrogation point. See **question mark.**

Interstate System (of highways) may be used in first references instead of the full name, National System of Interstate and Defense Highways.

intra-. intra-atomic, intramural, intrastate.

Intracoastal Waterway.

i.o.u.

Iowa. Do not abbreviate after cities and towns.

I.Q. for intelligence quotient.

Iran (formerly Persia).

Iraqi (person and adj.).

Irish International Airlines.

IRBM for intermediate range ballistic missile.

Ireland (not *Eire*).

Irish setter.

Irish terrier.

Irish water spaniel.

Irish wolfhound.

I.R.O. for International Refugee Organization.

ironclad.

Iron Curtain.

irreparable.

IRT for Interborough Rapid Transit.

Isbrandtsen Company, Inc. For first references *an Isbrandtsen freighter, etc.,* will suffice.

Israeli (person and adj.).

Istanbul (formerly Constantinople).

Italian Line.

italic.

I.T.O. for International Trade Organization.

I.T. & T. for International Telephone and Telegraph Corporation.

Ivy League.

J

jack-in-the-box.

Jack-of-all-trades.

jailer.

Jan. for January before numerals: *Jan. 10.*

Jap. Do not use as a synonym for Japanese.

Japan Air Lines.

Japanese spaniel.

jaywalker.

J.D. for Doctor of Law(s).

jeep. Lower-case when referring to the military vehicle; capitalize when referring to the civilian vehicle so trademarked.

Jehovah's Witnesses.

Jerseyan (person).

Jesus. Since this is a historical name and is correct in all cases, it is the preferred form. But in direct or indirect quotations and in matter directly concerning the Christian religion, *Christ* is also proper and should not be changed.

jet, jetliner. The first may be used as adjective or noun in writing about any pure-jet plane (no propellers). The second may be used for an airliner that is a pure jet. See **turbo-prop.**

jetport.

jg. for junior grade. Lieut. (jg.) John P. Manley.

jib (sail).

jibe. It has two meanings. One is to agree; the other, which is nautical, is to shift.

Joint Chiefs of Staff, the Joint Chiefs.

José.

Jr. for Junior in names. It is not preceded by a comma: *John P. Manley Jr.* (or *Sr.*). Also: *John P. Manley 2d.*

J.S.D. or **S.J.D.** for Doctor of Law.

Judge John P. Manley, the judge.

July. Do not abbreviate.

June. Do not abbreviate.

junior (class and member of that class).

jury room.

Justice John P. Manley, the justice.

K

Kan. for Kansas after cities and towns.

Kansas City Southern Railway.

keen-. keen-edged, keen-sighted, keen-witted.

keeshond, keeshonds.

Kerry blue terrier.

ketch. A two-masted vessel with the mizzen (the small mast aft) stepped forward of the yacht's waterline. See **yawl.**

key-. keyboard, keynote, keystone. But: key ring.

Khartoum.

kickoff (n.).

kidnap (v. only), **kidnapped, kidnapping, kidnapper.**

Kill van Kull.

kilowatt-hours.

kimono, kimonos.

kin is a collective word; one person is a *kinsman* or a *kinswoman*.

kind. It is *that kind, those kinds*.

kind of. It is wrong to say, *I like that kind of an apple*. Omit the *an*.

King Henry VIII, the King, Henry VIII, and sometimes Henry. Capitalize *His Majesty* and *His Royal Highness*, but use only in quoted matter.

King Charles spaniel.

King James Version (of the Bible).

KLM Royal Dutch Airlines. For first references a *KLM airliner, etc.*, will suffice.

knee-. kneecap, knee-deep, knee-high, kneepad.

knockdown (n.), **knockout** (n.).

Kodak (trademark).

Korean names. The Chinese practice of putting family names first is followed in some Korean names: *Kim* in a second reference to Kim Il Sung. But, unlike Chinese practice, the given names (Il Sung) are not hyphenated. Some Koreans, like Syng-

man Rhee, have westernized their names. Rhee is the family name.

krona, kronor (sing. and pl., Swedish money).

krone, kroner (sing. and pl., Danish and Norwegian money).

Ku Klux Klan (K.K.K.).

Kuomintang. It is the Kuomintang, not the Kuomintang party. *Tang* means party.

Ky. for Kentucky after cities and towns.

L

La. for Louisiana after cities and towns.

labeled.

"La Bohème."

Labrador retriever.

Lady. This title is applied to the wives of British knights, baronets, barons, viscounts, earls and marquesses. It is also applied to women below the rank of duchess who are peeresses in their own right: *the Countess of Cromartie, Lady Cromartie*. When applied to any one of those ranks, the title is never followed by a given name: *Lady Jellicoe*, not *Lady Patricia Jellicoe*.

The title is followed by a given name when it is applied to the daughters of earls, marquesses and dukes: *Lady Mary Grosvenor, Lady Mary*. But never *Lady Grosvenor*. The title is followed by the husband's given name when applied to the wives of the younger sons of marquesses and dukes: *Lady Malcolm Douglas-Hamilton*. In second references, it is *Lady Malcolm,* never *Lady Douglas-Hamilton.*

If a peeress in her own right or a peer's daughter marries, her title does not apply to her husband; if she outranks him she keeps her title: *the Countess of Cromartie and her husband, Lieut. Col. Edward Walter Blunt-Mackenzie.* Another example: *Lady Pamela Berry and her husband, Michael Berry.*

The form *Nancy Viscountess Astor* or *Anne Lady Orr Lewis* is used for widows and divorced women. In second references it is *Lady Astor* and *Lady Orr Lewis,* but never *Lady Nancy Astor* or *Lady Anne Orr Lewis.*

To distinguish between persons of the same name, use the form *Lady (Elizabeth) Jones;* or *Lady Jones, the former Elizabeth Smith;* or *Lady Jones, wife of Sir John Jones;* but never *Lady Elizabeth Jones,* except for the daughters of earls, marquesses and dukes.

La Guardia Airport.

laissez-faire.

lamb's-wool (adj.).

lamppost.

Lance Cpl. John P. Manley, Corporal Manley, the corporal.

land-. landfall, landlocked, landmark, landholder, landowner, land-poor, landslide.

languor.

lasso, lassos.

Lastex (trademark).

Latin America, Latin American (person), **Latin-American** (adj.).

latitude and longitude. Abbreviate: *Lat. 49 degrees N., Long. 24 degrees W.*

Latter-day Saints. See **Mormon.**

laughing-stock.

Laurel Race Course. But it is *a racecourse.*

law-. law-abiding, lawbreaker, lawmaker, lawsuit.

lay-. layman, layoff (n.), layout (n.).

lazybones.

lazy susan.

lean-to.

leatherneck (a marine).

leave-taking.

left(-). left field, left fielder, left guard, left-handed, leftover.

left, leftist, left wing. Do not capitalize *left* unless the political divisions in a country are formally designated as *the Left, the Right, etc.,* or the word appears in a party name. Do not capitalize *leftist* unless the reference is to such a division or party, or to a member of it. Do not capitalize *left wing* or *left-wing* (adj.) unless the reference is to such a political party or movement.

Left Bank (Paris).

legation. Lower-case when standing alone. But: *the Israeli Legation, the United States Legation.*

legionnaire.

legislative branch (of the United States Government). Also: *executive branch.*

Legislature. Capitalize when referring to the legislative body of a specific state.

Lehigh Valley Railroad.

Leif Ericson (the explorer).

Leiv Eiriksson Square (Brooklyn).

Lent, Lenten.

lèse-majesté.

letter(-). letter carrier, letterhead, letter man (sports), letter-perfect.

letters that appear in the body of a news story should be set in 8-point indent and not be quoted. Letters printed as texts should be similarly treated, but a letter that appears within the body of an indented text should be quoted or set double indent. Letters should follow this style, with the signature in caps and small caps.

> Dear Mr. Lincoln:
>> Tugwell, in his famous Los Angeles speech, said, etc.
>> Can you not do something?
>>> Sincerely yours,
>>> W. CLEVELAND RUNYAN.

Letters to The Times or the drama editor, music editor, sports editor, etc., are set full measure. Set dates at the left below the signature and indent 1 em unless otherwise instructed. Should the date make more than one line, set first line full and indent the turnover 1 em. The year must always go with the bottom date.

> SAMUEL OSGOOD CHASE.
> Stamford, Conn., Oct. 9, 1961.

Omit City in New York datelines. Omit N. Y. after Brooklyn. Long Island dates should read *Hempstead, L.I.* Staten Island dates should read *St. George, S.I.*

The style for salutations varies according to the section of the paper in which the letter appears. The complimentary close (*Yours very truly*) should be omitted.

Run up signatures to the last line of reading whenever there is room for 2 ems between, unless otherwise ordered:

> losses.   EDWARD A. FILENE.
> Columbus, Ohio, Oct. 10, 1961.

letup (n.).

level-headed.

Levi's (trademark).

L. I. for Long Island after cities and towns. It may also be used as noun and adjective in headlines if necessary.

liaison.

liberal. Do not capitalize as noun or adjective unless the reference is to a political party or movement so named or to a member of such a group.

liberal-minded.

Liberty Island. Formerly Bedloes Island.

Lieut. John P. Manley, Lieutenant Manley, the lieutenant.

Lieut. Col. John P. Manley, Colonel Manley, the colonel.

Lieut. Comdr. John P. Manley, Commander Manley, the commander.

Lieut. Gen. John P. Manley, General Manley, the general.

Lieut. Gov. John P. Manley (of a state), Lieutenant Governor Manley, the Lieutenant Governor.

life-. lifeboat, lifelike, lifelong, life-preserver, life-size, lifetime, lifework.

light-, -light. lighthearted, lighthouse, lightship, lightweight, light-year. Also: firelight, flashlight, gaslight, highlight, lamplight, limelight, searchlight, sidelight, sunlight.

likable.

like-, -like. like-minded, like-natured, likewise. Also: businesslike, ladylike, lifelike, shell-like.

lily of the valley.

Limburger (cheese).

linage (number of lines), **lineage** (descent).

Lincoln's Birthday (holiday).

line-, -line. lineman (football player), linesman (sports official), line-up (n.). Also: airline, balkline, breadline, coastline, deadline, shoreline, sideline, skyline, streamline, waistline.

Linotype (trademark).

lira, lire (sing. and pl., Italian money).

lists of names. See **casualty lists.**

literally. It is often used when *figuratively* is meant: *The Communist leaders in China are literally walking a tightrope.* Even when used correctly, it is usually superfluous.

littérateur.

Litt.D. or **D.Litt.** for Doctor of Literature.

living room (n.), **living-room** (adj.).

LL.B. for Bachelor of Laws.

LL.D. for Doctor of Laws.

Lloyd's (insurance), **Lloyds** (bankers).

loan. Avoid as a verb.

loath (unwilling), **loathe** (to hate).

localities and regions. Capitalize the names of specific localities and regions: *City of London* (financial district), *Left Bank, East Side, Middle West, Corn Belt.* Such designations are listed separately and alphabetically.

lock-. lockjaw, lockout (n.), locksmith, lockup (n.).

logrolling.

long-. longboat, long-drawn-out, long-haired, longhand, longshoreman, long-suffering, long-winded.

Long Island Rail Road, the Long Island, the L.I.R.R.

longitude. See **latitude and longitude.**

longshoreman. A longshoreman is a waterfront laborer. A stevedore, in waterfront usage, is an employer.

lookout (n.)

Loop (Chicago).

Lord. This British title is borne by barons, viscounts, earls and marquesses. Use it in first references to barons (*Lord Beaverbrook*) and in second references to the others. When applied to any of the four ranks, the title is never followed by a given name. It is followed by a given name when applied to the younger sons of marquesses and dukes: *Lord Charles Cavendish, Lord Charles,* but never *Lord Cavendish.*

Lord & Taylor.

Lotos Club.

Louisville & Nashville Railroad.

lowbrow.

Lower California (Mexico).

Lower East Side (of New York).

low mass. It is said, not sung. See **mass.**

LSI (landing ship infantry), **LST** (landing ship tank).

Lufthansa German Airlines. For first references *a Lufthansa airliner, etc.*, will suffice.

lunchroom.

luster.

Lutheran Church in America. A union (effective in 1962) of the American Evangelical Lutheran Church, the Augustana Evangelical Lutheran Church, the Finnish Evangelical Lutheran Church of America (Suomi Synod) and the United Lutheran Church in America.

Luxembourg (country, Paris gardens and museum).

Lykes Bros. Steamship Company, Inc. For first references *a Lykes Bros. freighter, etc.*, will suffice.

Lyons (France).

M

M.A. for Master of Arts. Also: *a master's degree.*

Macdougal Street (Manhattan), **McDougal Street** (Brooklyn).

machine gun (n.), **machine-gun** (adj.). Also: *submachine gun.*

Macy's. This is the style for all the stores of R. H. Macy & Co.

mad-. madcap, madhouse, madman.

madras (fabric).

magazines. Do not quote their names. Quote titles of magazine articles.

Magistrate John P. Manley, the magistrate.

Magna Carta does not require the article: *He cited Magna Carta.*

maidservant.

mailman.

Maine Central Railroad.

maître d'hôtel.

Maj. John P. Manley, Major Manley, the major.

Maj. Gen. John P. Manley, General Manley, the general.

Majlis (Iranian national assembly).

major-domo.

majority leader. Capitalize only when it precedes a name: *Senator John P. Manley, the majority leader; Majority Leader John P. Manley.*

make-. make-believe, makeshift, make-up (n. and adj.).

Man. for Manitoba after cities and towns.

mandatary (n.), **mandatory** (adj.).

maneuver.

maneuvers (military). Special designations of forces for purposes of a maneuver are set thus: *Blue fleet, Red army.*

manhattan (cocktail).

mannequin. A live model or a dummy used to display women's clothes.

man-of-war.

manpower.

mantel (shelf), **mantle** (cloak).

many-. many-hued, manyfold, many-sided.

Mao Tse-tung.

Marble Collegiate Reformed Church.

March. Do not abbreviate.

Marchioness of Milford-Haven, the; Lady Milford-Haven, the Marchioness. Use the non-English equivalents *Marquise* and *Marchesa* where appropriate.

Mardi Gras.

Marine Corps, Marines, marines. Capitalize *Marines* as a synonym for the United States Marine Corps; *He enlisted in the Marines. The Marines have landed.* But: *three marines, a company of marines.* Also: *the corps.*

Marquess of Milford-Haven, the; Lord Milford-Haven, the Marquess. Use the non-English equivalents *Marquis* and *Marchese* where appropriate. Also: *Marquis of Queensberry rules.*

Marseilles (France).

Marshal of the Royal Air Force Viscount Portal of Hungerford, Viscount Portal, Lord Portal. This is a rank that cannot properly be shortened. Holders of the rank usually have other titles by which they can be called. *R. A. F. Marshal* is not correct.

Marshall Plan.

martini (cocktail).

Mason-Dixon line. This short form is preferred to *Mason and Dixon's line.*

mass (religious). Lower-case *mass, high mass, low mass, requiem mass, etc.* High mass is sung, low mass is said. Masses are not *held* and do not *take place*; they may be *offered* or *celebrated.*

Mass. for Massachusetts after cities and towns.

masterful (overpowering), **masterly** (skillful).

Master Gunnery Sgt. John P. Manley, Sergeant Manley, the sergeant.

master sergeant. See **M. Sgt.**

mastiff.

Matamoras (Tex.), **Matamoros** (Mexico).

Matawan (N.J.), **Mattawan** (Mich.), **Matewan** (W. Va.), **Matteawan** (N.Y.).

matériel.

MATS for Military Air Transport Service.

Matson Navigation Company. For first references *a Matson liner, etc.,* will suffice.

matter-of-fact (adj.), **matter-of-course** (adj.).

matzoh.

May. Do not abbreviate.

Mayor John P. Manley, the Mayor.

mayoral (adj.), **mayoralty** (n.).

M.D. for Doctor of Medicine.

Md. for Maryland after cities and towns.

Me. for Maine after cities and towns.

Meadow Brook (L.I.), **Meadowbrook** (Philadelphia).

meager.

mean-. mean-souled, meantime, meanwhile. But: mean time (astronomical).

medals. Capitalize *Congressional Medal of Honor, Bronze Star, Purple Heart, Victoria Cross,* etc.

medieval.

melee.

memento, mementos.

memorandums.

Memorial Day (Decoration Day).

ménage.

merchant marine. Lower-case: *United States merchant marine.* Also lower-case titles of merchant marine officers when standing alone.

Mercurochrome (trademark).

merino, merinos.

Merrimack. The name of the Confederate ironclad is spelled with a *k.*

merry-go-round.

Met for Metropolitan Opera.

meter.

Methodist Church (not *Methodist Episcopal*).

Metropolitan (church title). Capitalize when used with name and when standing alone if referring to a specific individual.

metropolitan district (in sports).

Mexico City (not *Mexico, D. F.*).

Mich. for Michigan after cities and towns.

mid-. mid-air, mid-America, mid-Atlantic, mid-channel, mid-continent, midday, mid-ocean, midship, midstream, midsummer, midtown, midway, midweek, Midwest, midwife.

middle-. middle-aged, middleman, middle-of-the-road (adj.), middleweight.

Middle Ages.

Middle Atlantic States.

Middle East, Mideast. Use Middle East in stories. Either may be used in headlines. Do not use Near East. The Middle East comprises Cyprus, Iran, Iraq, Israel, Jordan, Lebanon, Saudi Arabia, the Sudan, Syria, United Arab Republic (Egypt), Yemen and Arab principalities.

Middle West, Midwest. For uniformity's sake, Middle West is preferred in references in stories to that section of the United States. Either form may be used in headlines.

Middle Western States.

Midshipman John P. Manley, Midshipman Manley, the midshipman.

Midwest Stock Exchange.

MIG for the Soviet airplane. Plural: MIG's.

Military Academy (United States), the Academy, West Point.

military ranks are listed separately and alphabetically.

militia. Lower-case when standing alone; capitalize when part of a name: *Naval Militia.*

mill-, (-)mill. millowner, millpond, millrace. Also: flour mill, gristmill, paper mill, pepper mill, sawmill, textile mill, windmill.

millennium.

-minded. air-minded, high-minded, money-minded, open-minded.

minesweeper.

minister (clerical title). It may be used in references to Baptist clergymen, who may also be called pastor, and to Congregationalists, Methodists and Unitarians: *the Rev. John P. Manley, minister of, etc.* See **pastor, rector.**

Minister of Justice John P. Manley; John P. Manley, Minister Without Portfolio; the Minister.

Minn. for Minnesota after cities and towns.

minority leader. Capitalize only when it precedes a name: *Senator John P. Manley, the minority leader; Minority Leader John P. Manley.*

Miss. *See* **Mr., Mrs., Miss.**

Miss. for Mississippi after cities and towns.

missile age.

missing antecedent. Pronouns require nouns as antecedents. An adjective will not serve: *The bitterness of the German resistance indicated their awareness of the danger.* But making it *the Germans' resistance* gives *their* its needed antecedent.

Missouri-Kansas-Texas Railroad, the Katy.

Missouri Pacific Railroad, the Mopac.

mitigate, which means to ease or lessen, is frequently confused with *militate,* which means to have weight or effect, usually against.

mix-up (n.).

Mo. for Missouri after cities and towns.

mockingbird.

Moderator (church title). Capitalize when used with name and when standing alone if referring to a specific individual.

Modernist (religious designation).

Mohammed (not *Mahomet*).

Mohawk Airlines.

mold.

molt.

money. Except for dollars and cents, and pounds, shillings and pence, symbols and abbreviations are not to be used in giving sums of money. The monetary unit is to be used following the figures: *10,000 pesos, 30,000 lire.* The exceptions are discussed separately and alphabetically.

mongoose, mongooses.

monkey wrench.

Monon Railroad.

monsignor. See **Msgr.**

Mont. for Montana after cities and towns.

Monterey (Calif.), **Monterrey** (Mexico).

months. Abbreviate January (Jan.), February (Feb.), August (Aug.), September (Sept.), October (Oct.), November (Nov.) and December (Dec.) in datelines and ordinary reading matter when followed by numerals: *Jan. 1, Feb. 16.* Do not abbreviate March, April, May, June and July.

moonlight. Do not quote when used to mean working at an additional job. Also: moonlighter, moonlighting.

Moore-McCormack Lines.

Moravian Church in America.

Mormon. The church is the Church of Jesus Christ of Latter-day Saints. It is headed by a President. This title and those of Elder, Presiding Bishop and Bishop should be capitalized in all specific references. It is proper to call members of the church Mormons, and the church the Mormon church, in second references.

Moslem. Use *Muslim* only when it appears in names of certain organizations in the United States and when referring to their members.

mosquito, mosquitoes.

Most Rev. This is the proper form for Roman Catholic Archbishops and Bishops: *the Most Rev. John P. Manley, Archbishop* (or *Bishop*) *of, etc.* It is also used for Archbishops of the Church of England. In second references: *the Archbishop, the Bishop.*

mother-. mother-in-law, motherhood, motherland. But: mother tongue.

Mother's Day.

motion pictures. In ordinary matter, quote their titles and capitalize principal words.

motor-. motorboat, motorcar, motorcycle, motorman.

Mount. Capitalize in ordinary reading matter when part of a name: *Mount Vernon.* The abbreviation (*Mt. Vernon*) may be used in headlines and in agate and other special matter.

mountain standard time (M.S.T.).

movements (music). Capitalize the names of movements: *the Scherzo, the Andante, etc.* Lower case if the movement is referred to by its place in the sequence: *the second movement, the finale.*

M.P. for Member of Parliament and military police.

m.p.h. for miles per hour. Do not use in ordinary reading matter, but spell out: *the speed limit is 65 miles an* (not *per*) *hour, a 45-mile-an-hour wind.* The abbreviation may be used in headlines.

Mr., Mrs., Miss. They are to be used not only for citizens of the English-speaking countries, but also for citizens of other countries who do not have royal, noble, military, religious or other titles of the kinds that replace the foreign equivalents of *Mr., Mrs.* and *Miss.*

The foreign equivalents — *M., Mme., Mlle.; Herr, Frau, Fräulein; Señor, Señora, Señorita; Senhor, Senhora, Senhorita; Signor, Signora Signorina, etc.*—may be used when desired for special effect, but not in the normal reporting of news. They also may be used in quoted matter if the words quoted were originally written or spoken in English. In translation of ordinary quoted matter into English, the foreign honorifics should be translated to *Mr., Mrs.* and *Miss.*

In general, *Mr.* is not used with the full name. It is used in second references to men of good standing. In general again, *Mr.* is not used with the names of persons who have been convicted of crime or who have unsavory reputations known without question to be deserved. But there may be exceptions, which must be carefully decided. When it is necessary to refer to a reputable and a disreputable person in close proximity, the discrimination should be avoided by using a pronoun or other identification for one man.

Mr. is not used with the names of sports figures in sports-section stories or in stories of sports contests that appear on Page 1. But if sports figures appear in general news stories, the *Mr.* is used. In the obituary of a sports figure, *Mr.* should be used in the passages relating to his birth, his death and any other circumstances not relating to his participation in his sport. But it would have been wrong, of course, to have said in Babe Ruth's obituary: *Having pointed out the target, Mr. Ruth hit one into the stands.*

Mr. is not needed with the names of persons of pre-eminence who are no longer living: *Newton, Lincoln, Lenin, Matisse, etc.* This is also true, especially in the arts, of some men still living. Matisse was one when he was alive. Reviewers and copy editors handling reviews will encounter the needless *Mr.* most often.

Some youths under 21 get the *Mr.*; some do not. The nature of the story is controlling.

Mrs. and *Miss* are a different case. They are to be used for all females, reputable or not, since they are needed to denote marital status.

Other titles used with personal names are listed separately and alphabetically. See also **personal names and nicknames.**

MS. for manuscript; MSS. in plural.

M.S. for Master of Science.

Msgr. John P. Manley, Monsignor Manley, the monsignor.

M. Sgt. John P. Manley, Sergeant Manley, the sergeant. Also: Senior (or Chief) M. Sgt. John P. Manley, etc.

multi-. multicolored, multifold, multiform, multilateral.

Muscle Shoals (Ala.).

music. Abbreviation, capitalization and punctuation guides are given in separate and alphabetical listings of various kinds of musical works and terms.

If the commonly used title of a work includes the instrumentation, the instrumentation is capitalized: *Bach's Suite No. 1 for Orchestra, Mozart's Piano Trio in B flat major (K. 254), Beethoven's Serenade for Flute, Violin and Viola (Op. 25).* If the instrumentation does not commonly appear in the title but is added to it for explanatory purposes, the names of the instruments are not capitalized: *Mozart's Sinfonia Concertante in E flat major* (the common title) *for violin and viola (K. 364).*

If the title contains a nickname, the nickname is quoted: *Beethoven's "Eroica" Symphony.* If the work has a special full title, all of it is quoted: *"Symphonie Fantastique," "Rhapsody in Blue."* In second references to specific compositions, lower-case *concerto, trio, quartet, symphony, suite, etc.*

N

naive, naiveté.

names of all sorts are listed separately and alphabetically. See also **abbreviations, apostrophe, Arab names, Arabic terms in place names, building names, Burmese names, Chinese names, company and corporation names, geographic names, Indonesian names, Korean names, Mr., Mrs., Miss, newspaper names, personal names and nicknames, plurals of proper names, Russian names, Spanish names, trademarks, Vietnamese names.**

Napoleon Bonaparte. But an accent is used in *Code Napoléon.*

napoleon (pastry).

NASA for National Aeronautics and Space Administration.

nation, national. Lower-case unless part of a formal name or title.

National Airlines.

National Baptist Convention of America.

National Baptist Convention, U. S. A., Inc.

National Capitol.

National Chairman (of a political party). John P. Manley, Republican National Chairman; the national chairman, the chairman.

National Council of Churches of Christ in the United States of America. The council itself approves a shorter version: National Council of Churches.

National Geographic Society. Do not confuse with the American Geographical Society.

National Guard. A member is a *guardsman* or a *National Guard man.*

National Institutes of Health.

nationalist. Capitalize only when it is part of the name of a political party or movement or when referring to a member of a group so named.

National Security Council, the Council.

nationwide.

natives. References to *the natives* are often offensive and should be avoided.

NATO for North Atlantic Treaty Organization.

Naval Academy (United States), the Academy, Annapolis.

Naval Militia (United States), the militia.

naval station. Capitalize only in full names: *Key West Naval Station, the naval station, the station.*

Navy. Capitalize in *United States Navy, British Navy, French Navy,* etc. It is *the Navy* in subsequent references to that of the United States, but lower-case such references to any foreign navy. It is also *Navy* in references to United States Naval Academy sports teams.

navy blue.

Navy ranks are listed separately and alphabetically. In addition to the familiar *seaman, yeoman, petty officer* and *chief petty officer* (which see), the Navy has a long list of other ratings. If, like the following examples, they are short enough and are recognizable as military titles, they may be used before the name and capitalized: *boatswain's mate, gunner's mate, radarman,* etc. Others are best used after the name and lower-cased: *aviation electronics technician, dental technician, machine accountant, patternmaker, storekeeper,* etc.

Nazi, Nazism.

N. B. for New Brunswick after cities and towns.

N.B.C. for National Broadcasting Company.

N. C. for North Carolina after cities and towns.

N. D. for North Dakota after cities and towns.

near-. nearby (adj., adv., prep.), near-side, nearsighted.

Near East. Do not use. See **Middle East.**

Neb. for Nebraska after cities and towns.

Nederland Line (N. V. Stoomvaart Maatschappij).

negligee.

Negro, Negroes.

nelson (wrestling hold). full nelson, three-quarters nelson, half nelson, quarter nelson.

nerve-racking.

Netherlands, the (not *Holland*).

Nev. for Nevada after cities and towns.

nevertheless.

new-. newcomer, newfangled, new-mown.

Newburgh (N. Y.).

Newfoundland (dog).

New Haven Railroad may be used instead of the official name, the New York, New Haven & Hartford Railroad Company, when necessary to avoid a cumbersome sentence.

New Orleans Cotton Exchange.

news-. newsletter, newsman, newsprint, newsstand.
But: news dealer.

New South Wales. Do not abbreviate after cities and towns.

newspaperman, newspaperwoman.

newspaper names. Do not quote them. Capitalize the article in the names of English-language and foreign-language papers: The Detroit Free Press, La Prensa. Also capitalize the article in second references: The Free Press. It is The Times of London, not *The London Times*.

The names of newspapers published in foreign languages should not be translated into English: Krasnaya Zvezda, not *Red Star;* Le Monde, not *The World*.

The following newspapers are members of the Publishers Association of New York:
The Daily News.
The New York Herald Tribune.
The New York Journal-American.
The Journal of Commerce.
The New York Mirror.

The New York Post.
The New York Times.
The New York World-Telegram and The Sun.
The Long Island Daily Press.
The Long Island Star-Journal.

New Testament.

New World (Western Hemisphere).

New Year's Day, New Year's Eve.

New York Airways.

New York Board of Rabbis. It represents the three branches of Judaism —Orthodox, Conservative and Reform.

New York Central Railroad, the Central.

New York, Chicago & St. Louis Railroad, the Nickel Plate.

New York City. But: *the city, the city government.*

New York Cocoa Exchange.

New York Coffee & Sugar Exchange.

New York Cotton Exchange.

New York International Airport may be called Idlewild Airport (which see).

New York, New Haven & Hartford Railroad Company may be called the New Haven Railroad (which see).

New York Mercantile Exchange.

New York Produce Exchange.

New York Stock Exchange.

New York, Susquehanna & Western Railroad, the Susquehanna.

New York Times, The. In stories, set The New York Times, The Times,

The New York Times Company (or Building), or any other form, in regular body type.

Nfld. for Newfoundland after cities and towns.

N. H. for New Hampshire after cities and towns.

nicknames. See **personal names and nicknames.**

night-. nightcap, nightclothes, nightdress, nightfall, nightgown, nightmare, nightstick, nighttime.

nineteen-thirties, etc. See **decades** and **years.**

N. J. for New Jersey after cities and towns.

N.L.R.B. for National Labor Relations Board.

N. M. for New Mexico after cities and towns.

No. for number. Do not use before schools, fire companies, lodges and similar units designated by numerals: *Public School 4* (or *P.S. 4*), *Hook and Ladder 16, Engine 4.* See **streets and avenues.**

nol-pros, nol-prossed.

no man's land.

non-. noncombatant, noncommissioned, noncommittal, noncompliance, nonconformist, nonexistent, nonpareil, nonpartisan, nonplus, nonresident, nonresistant, nonstop, nonunion.
But: non sequitur.

none. Construe as a plural unless it is desired to emphasize the idea of *not one* or *no one*—and then it is often better to use *not one* or *no one* instead of *none*.

nonetheless.

Norfolk & Western Railway.

North, north. Capitalize when referring to that geographic region of the United States; lower-case as a point of the compass. Also: *Far North.*

North German Lloyd.

North Jersey. This is an exception to the rule that calls for *northern New Jersey, eastern Indiana,* etc. Also: *South Jersey.*

North Pole. But: *the pole, polar.*

North Shore (L. I.). Also *South Shore.*

North Side. Capitalize when regularly used to designate a section of a city.

Northeast, northeast. Capitalize when referring to that geographic region of the United States; lower-case as a point of the compass.

Northeast Airlines.

Northern, northern. Capitalize when referring to the North (geographic region of the United States). But: *northern France, northern Ohio, northern half.*

Northerner. Capitalize when used to designate a native or inhabitant of the North (United States only).

Northern Pacific Railway.

Northwest, northwest. Capitalize when referring to that geographic region of the United States; lower-case as a point of the compass.

Northwest Airlines.

Norwegian America Line.

not only, but also. These words are often misplaced in a manner that destroys what should be a parallel construction: *It would not only be unwieldy but also unworkable.* Make it: *It would be not only unwieldy but also unworkable.* Omitting the *also* after the *but* often impairs the balance of the sentence.

notwithstanding.

Nov. for November before numerals: *Nov. 11.*

Novocain (trademark).

nowadays.

nowise (in no wise).

N. S. for Nova Scotia after cities and towns.

number of subject and verb. After *neither—nor,* if the subjects are both singular, use a singular verb: *Neither Jack nor Jill was happy.* If the subjects are both plural, use a plural verb: *Neither the Yankees nor the Athletics were hitting.* If one subject is singular and the other plural, use the number of the one following the *nor: Neither the man nor his horses were ever seen again.*

A copulative verb takes the number of the noun preceding it, which is the subject: *What was remarkable was the errors made on both sides.*

When the verb is far removed from the subject, and especially if another noun intervenes, mistakes like this one may occur: *The value of all of Argentina's exports to the United States are given as 183,000,-000 pesos.*

Improper identification of subject also causes trouble: *Natalie Gibbs is one of those women who goes in for fantastic dress.* The verb should be *go*, since its subject is *who*, which refers to the plural *women*.

Sums of money are usually construed as singular: *Ten dollars buys more now than five did then.* The thought here is of a sum, not of individual bills or coins. But the plural is used when the idea of individual items is suggested: *Three hundred parcels of food were shipped.*

Total of and *number of* may take either a plural or a singular verb: *A total of 102 persons were injured. A total of 500 pounds is needed. A number of persons were injured. The number of persons hurt was later found to be 12.*

If *couple* conveys the idea of two persons, it should be construed as a plural: *The couple were married.* But: *Each couple was asked to give $10.*

numbers. In general, spell out the first nine cardinal and ordinal numbers in ordinary reading matter: *He walked nine miles. There were eight applicants. He was the sixth. The game ended in the fifth inning.* Use figures for numbers above nine: *The table was set for 10. There were 50 in the audience. He owns 63 horses.*

The spelling-out-below-10 rule does not apply to the following:

Ages (which see).

Figures in headlines, financial and tabular matter.

Figures containing decimals (*3.4 inches of snow*). See **decimals.**

Statistics.

Results of voting. See **votes.**

Percentages. See **per cent.**

Sums of money. See **money.**

Times of day. See **time.**

Days of month. See **days.**

Latitude and longitude (which see).

Degrees of temperature. See **temperature.**

Dimensions, measurement and proportion (which see).

Numbers that are part of titles (*Chapter V, Article 6*).

Sports points, scores and times. See **sports.**

Although all round numbers of 10 and above are usually given in figures, there are occasions when spelling out is appropriate: *They planned to enlist a million workers. He said his opponent was one hundred per cent wrong. Fifty to sixty thousand voted.*

The rules for spelling out and for use of figures apply also to adjectival forms: *four-mile hike, 11-mile hike, five-day week, 40-hour week, five-ton truck, 9,000-ton ship, 3.5-inch snow.*

In ordinary reading matter, spell out all numbers that begin a sentence: *Five hundred delegates attended.* In series including both numbers that would ordinarily be spelled out and numbers that would ordinarily be given in figures, make the style conform: *4 submarines, 10 destroyers and 15 carriers; the 9th and 10th centuries.* This rule does not apply to streets and avenues.

In headlines, figures may be used for all cardinal and ordinal numbers except, in some cases, *1* and *1st*. *One Hurt* is preferred to *1 Hurt*, and *First Prize* to *1st Prize*. Likewise *First Aid*, not *1st Aid*. But *1-Cent Tax* (or *1c Tax*), *1 Per Cent* and similar constructions may be used.

Ordinal numbers are expressed in figures as follows: *2d, 3d, 4th, 11th, 21st, 33d, 124th.*

nursemaid.

nurseryman.

N. Y. for New York after cities and towns.

nylon.

O

O, oh. *O* is always capitalized, whether occurring at the beginning of a sentence or at some intermediate point: *For Thee, O Lord.* *Oh* is capitalized only when occurring at the beginning of a sentence: *But, oh, how glad we were.* The form *O* is virtually obsolete as far as ordinary usage is concerned and is found principally in quotations from poetry, in classical references and in religious matter.

O.A.S. for Organization of American States.

obbligato.

Occident, Occidental. Capitalize when referring to Europe or the Western Hemisphere or to an inhabitant of one of those regions.

Oct. for October before numerals: *Oct. 14.*

octavo, octavos.

octet. See **quartet** or **trio.**

odd-, -odd. odd-looking, odd-numbered, Also: 20-odd, 200-odd.

O.E.C.D. for Organization for Economic Cooperation and Development.

Off Broadway. *He is directing an Off Broadway play. A survey showed that Off Broadway was flourishing.* But: *The play was produced off Broadway.*

off-, -off. off-color, offhand, offshoot, offshore, offside. Also: layoff, playoff, stop-off, take-off (all n.).

office-. officeholder, officeseeker. But: office boy.

officials. Their titles are listed separately and alphabetically. See **company officers.**

offshore oil. Use instead of *tidelands oil* unless the deposits are in the area between the low-tide and high-tide marks.

Ohio. Do not abbreviate.

oil-. oilcloth, oilfield, oilman, oilskin, oilstove. But: oil burner.

O.K., O.K.'d, O.K.'s.

Okla. for Oklahoma after cities and towns.

old-. old-fashioned, old-school (adj.), old-timer.

Old English sheepdog.

Old Testament.

Old World.

Olympic Games, the games.

one-. one-piece (adj.), oneself, one-sided.

One Thousand Guineas (horse race).

onlooker.

only. Place it next to the word it modifies: *He ate only a sandwich,* not *He only ate a sandwich.* See **not only, but also.**

onside.

Ont. for Ontario after cities and towns.

open-. open-field (adj.), openhanded, openhearted, openwork.

opera. Capitalize and quote a title: *"Aïda" is an opera by Verdi.* The names of characters in operas should not be quoted: *Aïda, Carmen, Violetta, Mimi, etc.* Also: *opéra bouffe, Opéra-Comique, operagoer.* See **Met.**

opus (music). Abbreviate, capitalize and parenthesize in a title: *Chopin's Rondo in E flat major (Op. 16).* But: *His Opus 16 is moving.*

Opposition. Capitalize when referring to a definite political faction opposing the party in power in a foreign country if it is so designated in a formal sense: *The Opposition objected. The Opposition Labor party divided on the issue.*

orbit. It may be used as a transitive and intransitive verb: *The United States orbited a weather satellite. The satellite orbited.*

Ore. for Oregon after cities and towns.

Orient, Oriental. Capitalize when referring to Asia and the East or to an inhabitant of those regions. But: *an oriental rug.*

Orlon (trademark).

ORT, American Women's. In second references: ORT, without the article. ORT stands for Organization for Rehabilitation Through Training.

out-, -out. out-and-out, outboard, outbound, outclimb, outdo, outdoor, outfield, out-of-doors (adj.), outpatient, outrigger, outscore, outspoken, outtrade. Also: fallout (n.), hide-out, pullout (n.), walkout (n.).

Outer Seven (European Free Trade Association). Construe as a plural.

over-, -over. overabundant, overalls (outergarments), over-all (adj.), overexcitable, overproduction, overprompt, overindulgence, oversensitive, overexpand. Also, all n.: carry-over, change-over, hangover, holdover, take-over, turnover, walkover.

overture. Capitalize in a title: *Beethoven's "Egmont" Overture.* But: *a Beethoven overture.* Also capitalize when the overture is referred to the source: *the Overture to* (not *of*) *"La Gazza Ladra," by Rossini.*

oxford (cloth, shoes).

oxford blue.

oxford gray.

P

Pa. for Pennsylvania after cities and towns.

Pacific. The actual shoreline of the Pacific Ocean is the Pacific *coast;* the region of the United States lying along the shoreline is the Pacific *Coast,* the *West Coast,* or *the Coast.* Also: *Pacific Coast States, Pacific States, Pacific Northwest, North Pacific, South Pacific.*

Pacific Coast Stock Exchange.

Pacific Far East Line.

Pacific standard time. (P.S.T.)

page numbers. Capitalize only in references to pages in The New York Times: *Page 1, Page 18.* Lower-case such references to pages in other publications, books, etc. In special

71

matter, abbreviations may be used: *p. 5, 321 pp., pp. 19, 20 and 21.* Capitalize the abbreviations (*P.* and *PP.*) if the reference is to The Times.

paintings. Quote their titles; capitalize principal words.

Pakistani (person and adj.).

palate (part of mouth), **palette** (paint board), **pallet** (bed).

pallbearer.

Pan-. It is generally hyphenated: Pan-African, Pan-American (in the general sense), Pan-German, Pan-Slav. But: Pan American World Airways, Pan American Union.

Panagra (Pan American-Grace Airways).

Panamanian.

Pan American World Airways.

paneled.

panhandle.

panic-stricken.

papal. Lower-case unless part of a name or title.

Papal Nuncio. Capitalize when used with name and when standing alone if referring to a specific individual. A nuncio is a Roman Catholic representative accredited by the Pope to a foreign government. An apostolic delegate is accredited by the Pope to the church or hierarchy in a foreign country.

paper-. paperback, paper-backed, paper-bound, paperhanger, paperweight.

papier-mâché.

paralleled.

parentheses and brackets. In general, parentheses are used to indicate an interpolation by a writer in his own copy. If an editor makes an ordinary interpolation that the writer of a news story should have made but overlooked, parentheses should also be used: *The jury awarded £100 ($280) in damages.*

Use parentheses in Q. and A. matter when describing an action not directly a part of the interrogation: *Q. Will you kindly point out the figures? (handing the witness a list)—*

A nickname interpolated in an actual name should be enclosed in parentheses: *Anthony (Tough Tony) Anastasia.* The parentheses should also be used in making a differentiation such as this: *the Springfield (Mass.) General Hospital.*

When a clause in parentheses comes at the end of a sentence and is part of it, put the period outside the parentheses mark: *The witness did not identify the automobile (a Cadillac, according to earlier testimony).* If the parenthesized matter is independent of the sentence and requires a period, the period is placed inside the closing mark: *The university was not identified. (It developed later that he was speaking of Harvard.)*

Do not place a comma before a parenthesis mark; if a comma is indicated after the sentence or phrase preceding the parenthesis, the comma should be placed outside the closing parenthesis mark: *The university (Harvard), he said, was not involved.*

Do not use dash and parenthesis together.

Brackets, in general, are used to enclose an interpolation by an editor

72

or, in a datelined story, material from another place. Bracketed matter in a news story should be paragraphed and indented unless it is merely an interpolated phrase or a short sentence that may be interpolated without making the original paragraph cumbersome. Bracketed matter should not appear in a story not carrying a dateline; rather, the material should be woven into the story.

Time elements in bracketed material should be given as the specific day of the week, rather than as *yesterday* or *today*.

In quoted matter, the brackets are used in place of the parentheses to indicate that the person quoted did not make the interpolation. Such an interpolation in a news story thus might be made by either the writer of the story or by the editor: *"Then,"* he said, *"I went to see [Attorney General] Kennedy."*

parenthetical attribution. The interpolated phrase of attribution is often misused: *In Laos the State Department announced that two attachés were missing.* The phrase *the State Department announced* is a parenthesis, and does not govern the tense of the verb that follows. It should be set off by punctuation: *In Laos, the State Department announced, two attachés are missing.* Another example: *While the building was being renovated Mr. Brown said that the document had been found in a closet.* It should read: *While the building was being renovated, Mr. Brown said, the document was found in a closet.* Ignorance of a parenthesis may result in ambiguity: *In 1960 the witness testified that he never saw the defendant.* It

should read: *In 1960, the witness testified, he never saw the defendant.*

pari-mutuels (n.), **pari-mutuel** (adj.).

paris green.

Parliament. Capitalize in all specific references.

parliamentary.

parlormaid.

part-time (adj.).

party. Do not capitalize in *Republican party, Democratic party, Labor party, Communist party, etc.*

party designations of members of Congress and of state legislatures are given as follows: *Senator John P. Manley, Republican of New York; Assemblyman John P. Manley, Democrat of Buffalo.*

passenger-miles.

passer(s)-by.

Passover.

pass-. passbook, passkey, password.

past master.

pastor. As a title following a name, pastor may be used in referring to Lutherans, Baptists (who may also be called minister) and Roman Catholic clergymen in charge of parishes: *the Rev. John P. Manley, pastor of,* etc.; *the pastor.* Lutherans sometimes use Pastor before a name in second references: *Pastor Manley.* Local custom should be ascertained and followed. See **minister, rector.**

Paterson (N. J.), **Patterson** (N. Y.).

Patrolman John P. Manley, the patrolman.

73

pawn-. pawnbroker, pawnshop. But: pawn ticket.

pay-. pay-as-you-go (n. and adj.), payday, paymaster, payoff (n.), payroll.

peach Melba.

peccadillo, peccadillos.

peddler.

peer. A peer is a member of one of the five degrees of British nobility—baron, viscount, earl, marquess, duke (which see). The son or daughter of a peer who bears a courtesy title is not a peer. For example: *the Duke of Marlborough,* a peer; *the Marquess of Blandford,* his son; *the Earl of Sunderland,* his grandson.

To distinguish between peers of the same name, use the full title or territorial designation: *Viscount Alexander of Hillsborough and Earl Alexander of Tunis, Viscount Alexander and Earl Alexander.* When the names are not in juxtaposition, each may be called *Lord Alexander* in second references.

A special case: Some peers prefer to be known professionally by their family names: *Earl Russell, Lord Russell* or *Bertrand Russell,* but never *Lord Bertrand Russell* or *Mr. Russell.*

Peking (not *Peiping*).

Pekingese (dog).

Penal Code.

pendant (n.), **pendent** (adj.).

Pennsylvania Railroad, the Pennsy.

Pennsylvania - Reading Seashore Lines.

Pennsylvania Station.

penthouse.

people's democracy. Avoid the term unless it appears in a name or the context makes clear that it is a Communist definition.

per cent. In ordinary matter, it is always two words with no points and the number is always expressed in figures: *80 per cent, 8 per cent, one-half of 1 per cent.* But: *five percentage points, 12 percentage points.* The symbol % may be used with the figure in headlines and tabular matter: *5% Raise, 93%.*

père.

period. The various uses of the period are shown throughout in the separate and alphabetical listings. See especially **abbreviations.**

An important thing to remember about the period is that it is used to end a sentence and that the insertion of one can often mean two easy-to-read sentences instead of one cumbersome sentence.

Do not use the period after *per cent; 8vo, 12mo;* Roman numerals; serial references such as *(1)* and *(a);* sums of money in dollar denominations (set *$50* unless cents are added: *$50.69*); abbreviations for shillings and pence (set *9s, 3d*).

permissible.

Persia. The former name of Iran. Use only in references to the past.

Persian (not *Iranian*) is the principal language of Iran.

Persian lamb.

personal names and nicknames. Do not contract Christian names in writing and editing copy unless the person mentioned is known only by the contraction (*Alex, Ben, Fred, etc.*, without periods) or unless the name occurs in sports or other matter where nicknames are appropriate. Do not enclose nicknames in quotation marks: *John (Butch) Manley, Honest John Manley, Jack Manley, Jack the Ripper; John P. Manley, alias James Anderson.* But in letters written to The Times by readers, names and nicknames may in general be printed as received.

The particles *de, du, di, da, le, la, van, von, ter, etc.*, appear in many personal names: Although there are many exceptions, they are usually lower-cased in foreign names: *Charles de Gaulle.* They are usually capitalized in the names of United States citizens: *Martin Van Buren.* But again there are exceptions: *du Pont.* An individual's preference is to be respected.

Titles and ranks used with personal names are listed separately and alphabetically. See **Mr., Mrs., Miss,** which are to be used for citizens of all countries, and **Arab names, Burmese names, Chinese names, Indonesian names, Korean names, Russian names, Spanish names, Vietnamese names.**

personnel.

Pesach (Feast of Passover).

petit (not *petty*) larceny.

Petty Officer John P. Manley, Mr. (or Petty Officer) Manley, the petty officer.

Pfc. John P. Manley, Private Manley, the private.

pharmacopoeia.

Ph.D. for Doctor of Philosophy.

phenomenon, phenomena.

Philadelphia-Baltimore Stock Exchange.

Philadelphia Yearly Meeting of the Religious Society of Friends.

Photostat (trademark).

piano, pianos.

pick-. pick-me-up, pickpocket, pickup (n.).

pickets (not *picketers*).

picnic, picnicking.

pièce de résistance.

piecemeal.

pigeonhole (n. and v.).

pilotboat.

pince-nez.

Ping-Pong (trademark). The general term is *table tennis.*

pipeline.

pistol. A pistol is a hand weapon. It may be a revolver (which see) or an automatic pistol (which see).

Pittsburg (Kan.), **Pittsburgh** (Pa.).

Pittsburgh Stock Exchange.

Pittsburgh & Lake Erie Railroad.

Pittsburgh & West Virginia Railway.

Place. Spell out and capitalize in ordinary reading matter when part of a name: *Patchen Place.* The abbreviation (*Patchen Pl.*) may be used in headlines if necessary and in agate and other special matter.

place-kick (n.,v.,adj.), **place-kicker.**

place names. See **geographic names.**

plainclothes man.

plaque.

plaster of paris.

Plattsburgh (N. Y.).

play-. playbill, playhouse, playgoer, playoff, playwright.

play-by-play.

plays and revues. In ordinary matter, quote their titles and capitalize principal words.

pleaded innocent. Do not use in place of *pleaded not guilty.* Lawyers say there is a difference.

Plexiglass (trademark).

plow.

plurals of abbreviations, letters and figures. These plurals are usually formed by adding *'s,* as in *M.D.'s, C.P.A.'s, A B C's, p's and q's, size 8's.* However, plurals of some abbreviations are formed without using the apostrophe: *co-ops, vets* (for veterinarians, but not for veterans, except in AMVETS.)

plurals of combined words and compounds. These are variously formed. The plurals of military titles are for the most part formed by adding *s* to the second word, which is usually the more important element of the compound: *major generals, lieutenant colonels, etc.* But the *s* is added to the first word in *sergeants major.* In civilian titles the *s* is added to the first word, usually the more important element: *attorneys general, postmasters general, etc.* The *s* is also added to the more important element in words like *courts-martial* and *rights-of-way.* When compounds are written as one word, the plurals are formed in the normal way. This guide applies also to such words as *cupfuls, handfuls, tablespoonfuls, breakthroughs.*

plurals of common nouns. Ordinarily the plurals are formed by the addition of *s* or *es: hammers, saws, churches, boxes, gases.* Words ending in *o* preceded by a vowel take the *s: folios, taboos.* Words ending in *o* preceded by a consonant usually take *es: echoes, embargoes, Negroes* (always capitalized), *potatoes.*

Words ending in *y* preceded by a vowel take the *s* only: *alloys, attorneys, days.* When words end in *y* preceded by a consonant, the *y* is changed to *i* and *es* is added: *armies, ladies, skies.* See **plurals of proper names** for exceptions.

Some words are the same in the plural as in the singular: *chassis, deer, sheep, swine, fowl, etc.* The collective plural of *fish* is the same as the singular, but *fishes* may be used in denoting specific kinds: *certain fishes.*

The original plurals of some nouns of foreign derivation are to be used: *data, agenda* (which, however, may now also be used as a singular), *phenomena, etc.* The plurals of some other nouns of foreign derivation are formed in the normal English manner: *memorandums, curriculums, formulas, etc.*

plurals of proper names. The plurals of proper names are formed by adding *s* or *es: Cadillacs, Harolds, Joneses, Charleses.* In forming the plurals of proper names ending in *y,* the *y* is not changed to *ie* as it is in some common nouns: *Harrys, Kennedys, Germanys, Kansas Citys.* There are some exceptions, like *Alleghenies, Rockies, Sicilies.*

P.M. (time). Capitalize: *10:30 P.M.* yesterday. Avoid this redundancy: *10:30 P.M. last night.* Also: *10 P.M.,* not *10:00 P.M.*

pocket-. pocketbook, pocketknife.

poetry. In ordinary matter, quote the titles of poems and capitalize principal words. Poetry set in verse style does not require quotation marks.

point. See **period.**

Point. Spell out and capitalize in ordinary reading matter when part of a name: *Montauk Point.* The abbreviation *(Montauk Pt.)* may be used in headlines and in agate and other special matter.

point-blank.

pointer (dog).

points of the compass. Spell out in ordinary reading matter: *north, northeast, north-northeast, etc.* Abbreviations (without periods) may be used in ship news and yachting matter: *N, NE, NNE.* See **latitude and longitude.**

pole vault (n.), **pole-vault** (v.), **pole vaulter.**

Police Commissioner John P. Manley, the Commissioner.

Police Department, the department.

Police Headquarters, headquarters.

police stations. Lower-case, even when referring to a specific station: *47th Street station.*

policyholder.

Polish National Catholic Church of America.

political parties. Do not capitalize *party* in names: *Democratic party,* *Republican party, Communist party, Labor party, etc.* Capitalize designations of members: *Democrats, Republicans, Communists, Laborites.*

politicking.

Pomeranian (dog).

Pontiff. Capitalize when referring to a specific pope.

pontifical. Lower-case unless part of a name or title.

poodle.

Pope. Capitalize with a name *(Pope John XXIII)* or when standing alone if a specific individual is referred to.

portland cement.

Port-au-Prince (Haiti).

Port Chester (N. Y.).

Port of New York Authority.

Port of Spain (Trinidad).

possessive. See **apostrophe.**

post-. post-bellum (adj.), postclassic, post-Columbian, post-graduate, post-mortem, postnuptial, postwar.

post- (mail). postcard, postpaid, postroad, postman, postmaster. But: post office.

potpourri.

potter's field.

pounds, shillings and pence. The symbol £ is usually used with figures: *£15,000.* But, as with dollars, round numbers and indefinite sums may be spelled out: *half a million pounds, ten to eleven thousand pounds.* Spell out *shillings* and *pence* when they appear alone in sums: *3 shillings, twopence.* But detailed sums are set thus: *£16 4s 3d.*

Power Authority of the State of New York. But *State Power Authority* may be used in first references.

powerhouse.

P. & O.-Orient Lines.

P.P.R. for permanent personal registration.

P.R. for Puerto Rico after cities and towns.

Prairie States.

pre-. preadolescent, preconvention, predecease, predetermined, pre-empt, pre-emptory, pre-existent, prejudge, prenatal, pre-Roman, preview, prewar.

prefixes and suffixes. Words formed from them and from other combining forms will be found under the separate and alphabetical listings of the prefixes, suffixes and other combining words.

prelude (music). Capitalize in a title: *Chopin's Prelude in C sharp minor.* Also: *the Prelude to the Third Act of "Die Meistersinger."*

Premier. This is the title for the first minister in most countries not in the British Commonwealth, and for the heads of Canadian provinces. Use *Prime Minister* for the heads of the Commonwealth countries, including Canada, and of South Africa. Capitalize both titles in second references to specific individuals.

premiere.

Presbyterian Church in the U. S. (Southern).

Presidency. Capitalize when the reference is to the office of the President of the United States.

President Manley (of the United States or, with first name, of a foreign government), the President. But: *John P. Manley, president of the Ford Motor Company; the president of the company.*

President-elect John P. Manley, President-elect Manley, the President-elect (of a national government; otherwise lower-case).

Presidential. Capitalize when the reference is to the President of the United States or to his office.

President of the Board of Trade is a British Cabinet title and *President* should be capitalized when the full title is given.

President pro tem (of the Senate).

prevent. This is disapproved: *The police tried to prevent him jumping.* Make it either *prevent him from jumping* or *prevent his jumping.*

priest. Do not capitalize when directly following a name or in second references.

prima-facie (adj.).

Primary Day.

Prime Minister. This is the title for the first minister in Britain and other countries of the British Commonwealth, and in South Africa. Use *Premier* for other countries having a similar system. Capitalize both titles in second references to specific individuals.

Prince Charles, the Prince.

Princes Bay (S.I.).

Prince Edward Island. Do not abbreviate after cities and towns.

Principal John P. Manley, Principal Manley, the principal.

private (military rank). See **Pvt.**

private first class. See **Pfc.**

prizefight.

pro-. pro-Arab, proclassical, pro-French, proslavery.

Prof. John P. Manley, Professor Manley, the professor. Also: John P. Manley, *professor of history* (or *chairman of the department of history*). But if he holds a special chair: John P. Manley, *the Ebenezer Benton Professor of History.*

programed, programing.

propeller.

proper names. Proper names of all sorts are listed separately and alphabetically.

prophecy (n.), **prophesy** (v.).

protégé (m.), **protégée** (f.).

Protestant churches are listed separately and alphabetically.

Protestant Episcopal Church. *Episcopal* by itself may be used in second references if the context is clear.

proved (not *proven*).

provided. Use *provided,* not *providing,* in the sense of *if*: *He will make the trip, provided he gets a week off.*

proviso, provisos.

provost marshal.

P. S. for Public School. Do not use *No.* before the numeral: *P. S. 29.* The preferred form is *Public School 29,* but *P.S.* is often more appropriate: *good old P. S. 10.*

PT boat for motor torpedo boat.

Puerto Rico.

pug (dog).

punctuation is discussed under **colon, comma, dash, ellipsis, exclamation mark, hyphen, parentheses and brackets, period, question mark, quotation marks, semicolon.**

Purim (Feast of Lots).

pussyfoot.

putout (n.).

Pvt. John P. Manley, Private Manley, the private.

PX for post exchange.

pygmy.

Q

Qantas Empire Airways.

Quai d'Orsay.

Quakers. Their chief organization in the United States is the Society of Friends.

quarter-. quarterback, quarter-deck, quartermaster, quarterstretch. But: quarter horse.

quartet. Capitalize in the title of a musical work: *Brahms's Quartet No. 3 in E flat major (Op. 67), Schubert's "Death and the Maiden" Quartet.* Capitalize in the name of an ensemble: *the Budapest String Quartet.* But: *a new quartet, a quartet of singers.*

quarto, quartos.

quasi(-). A separate word when used with a noun: *quasi comfort.* Hyphenate when used with adjective, adverb or verb: *quasi-judicial.*

Que. for Quebec after cities and towns.

Queen Elizabeth II, the Queen, Elizabeth II and sometimes Elizabeth. Capitalize *Her Majesty* and *Her Royal Highness,* but use only in quoted matter.

Queensboro Bridge.

question mark. It is used to indicate a direct query: *What are the problems facing the country?* Indirect questions do not require the mark: *They asked if he could attend.* Requests cast in the form of questions also take the period rather than the question mark: *Will you please register at the desk. May I take your coat.* See **quotation marks.**

questionnaire.

queue (line of persons).

quick-. quick-fire (adj.), quicklime, quicksand, quicksilver, quick-witted.

quintet. See **quartet** or **trio.**

quotation marks. Quoted matter in stories, spoken or written, is enclosed in double (outside) or single (inside) quotation marks: *"I do not know the meaning you attach to 'work week,' " he said. "Please tell me."*

In headlines and subheads the single mark is used: *JONES PROTESTS 'UNFAIR' CHARGES.*

The period and the comma should be placed inside the quotation marks, as in the first of the foregoing examples. The colon and the semi-colon are placed outside: *He defined "work week": the average number of hours worked weekly by the men in his factory.* Question marks and exclamation marks may come before or after the quotation marks, depending on the meaning: *The crowd shouted, "Long live the King!" Just imagine, he was afraid of "elephants without trunks"! "Who are these 'economic royalists'?" he asked. Have you read "Lord Jim"?*

In continuous quoted matter that is more than one paragraph long, place quotation marks at the beginning of each of the paragraphs and at the end of the last paragraph only.

Do not quote Q. and A. matter or dialogue in which each paragraph begins with the name of the person speaking. Do not quote texts or textual excerpts (except, of course, quotations within a text) that are carried in textual form.

In general, the use of slang words should be justified by the context and should not require quotation marks. But the marks should be used with words or phrases employed in an arbitrary or opposite sense.

Guides for the use of quotation marks are given throughout in the separate and alphabetical listings.

R

Rabbi John P. Manley, Rabbi Manley, the rabbi.

Rabbinical Assembly of America. A Conservative group.

Rabbinical Council of America. An Orthodox group.

race-. racecourse, racegoer, raceway. But: race horse, race track.

radio-. radioactive, radioactivity, radiogram, radio-isotope, radioman, radiophone.

R.A.F. for Royal Air Force.

railroad man, railway man.

railroads. The principal railroads in the United States and Canada are listed separately and alphabetically.

rain-. raincoat, rainfall, rainproof, rain-soaked, rainstorm.

raise. Use instead of *rise* for increase in pay: *He received a $10 raise.* But not this redundancy: *He received a $10 pay raise.*

raison d'être.

rape. It is preferred to *criminal attack, criminal assault, sexual attack* and other imprecise terms.

rapid-fire (adj.).

rapprochement.

rate. birth rate, death rate, insurance rate, interest rate, tax rate.

rayon.

R.C.A. for Radio Corporation of America.

re-. reappear, reconstruct, recover (regain), re-cover (cover again), re-elect, re-election, re-enter, re-entry, reform (change for the better), re-form (form again), remake, reopen.

R.E.A. for Rural Electrification Administration.

REA Express (formerly Railway Express Agency).

Reading Company (railroad).

ready. Avoid as a verb.

ready-. ready-made (n. and adj.), ready-to-wear (n. and adj.).

realtor. This is a designation for a real-estate man belonging to a local board affiliated with the National Association of Real Estate Boards.

Rear Adm. John P. Manley, Admiral Manley, the admiral.

rear guard (n.), **rear-guard** (adj.).

recherché (adj.).

reconnaissance.

Recruit John P. Manley, the recruit.

rector is to be used in referring to a Protestant Episcopal clergyman in charge of a parish: *the Rev. John P. Manley, rector of, etc.* See **minister, pastor.**

Red. Capitalize as noun or adjective when used as a synonym for Communist. To avoid confusion, especially in headlines, do not use as synonym for a Russian or, in the plural, for the Soviet Union's Government. But *Red nations* (including the Soviet Union) is all right.

referable.

referendums.

Reform, Reformed. Various Jewish synagogues and organizations are Reform (not *Reformed*) groups, e.g., the Association of Reform Rabbis of America. Various Christian churches have *Reformed* in their names.

Reformed Church in America.

Regents, Board of; the Regents.

regime.

regiment (military). Do not abbreviate: *Fifth Regiment, 13th Regiment, etc.; the regiment.*

regions. Geographic regions are listed separately and alphabetically.

Regular Army (of the United States).

reinforce.

relative. Use *relative*, not *relation*, for a person.

religion. Religious holidays, organizations, titles, etc., are listed separately and alphabetically.

Renaissance. Capitalize when referring to the movement and the period that followed the medieval period. Lower-case in its general meaning: *a renaissance of poetry.*

repertory (not *repertoire*).

Representative John P. Manley, Democrat of Utah; the Representative (if he is a member of Congress or of a state legislature). Do not abbreviate, except in headlines: Rep. Manley.

representative at large. No hyphens. Capitalize if it is a governmental title: *Representative at Large.*

Representative-elect John P. Manley, the Representative-elect.

Republic. Capitalize when used alone if the United States is meant.

Republican National Convention, the national convention, the convention.

Republican party.

requiem mass.

Reserve(s). Capitalize the *Active Reserve, Air Force Reserve, Army Reserve, Enlisted Reserve, Naval Reserve, Organized Reserve Corps, Ready Reserve,* etc. Also: *the Reserve, the Reserves, Reserve officer.* But: *a reservist, the reserves* (meaning men, rather than organizations).

resin.

restaurateur.

result of. Use *as a result of* rather than *as the result of.* There may be more than one result.

résumé.

retired. Do not abbreviate or capitalize in denoting military status: *Col. John P. Manley, retired.* Sometimes, especially if the person is well known, it is not necessary to give the retirement status in the first reference. It may be worked in later, in a more graceful manner: *General Clay, who retired from the Army in 1949, is chairman of the Continental Can Company.*

retriever (dog).

Reuters. In stories it is *Reuters,* without an article, or *the news agency Reuters.* Also, in datelines: LONDON, Jan. 10 (Reuters)—etc. Use agate credit line above the dateline on Page 1 stories:

By Reuters

Rev. John P. Manley, the; Mr. Manley or Father Manley, depending upon the church. Never use *Rev.* without *the* except in headlines. Always use the given name or initials after *Rev.,* even in headlines. *Mr.* is to be used instead of *the Rev. Mr.* in second references. See **Father, minister, pastor, rector.**

Rev. Dr. John P. Manley, the; Dr. Manley.

revolver. A revolver is a hand weapon with a revolving chamber that holds the cartridges. It is different from an automatic pistol, which has a magazine that holds the cartridges. Both are properly called pistols.

R.F.D. for rural free delivery.

rhapsody. Capitalize in a title: *Brahms's Rhapsody in E flat (Op. 119).* Quote if part of a title that is assigned to the work by a composer and goes beyond a mere description of the kind of work: *Gershwin's "Rhapsody in Blue."*

rhinoceros, rhinoceroses.

R. I. for Rhode Island after cities and towns.

RIAS for Radio in American Sector (of Berlin).

Richmond, Fredericksburg & Potomac Railroad.

Riddle Airlines.

riffraff.

right, rightist, right wing. Do not capitalize *right* unless the political divisions in a country are formally designated as *the Right, the Left, etc.*, or the word appears in a party name. Do not capitalize *rightist* unless the reference is to such a division or party, or to a member of it. Do not capitalize *right wing* or *right-wing* (adj.) unless the reference is to such a division or party.

right(s)-of-way.

Right Rev. is the proper form for Bishops of the Protestant Episcopal Church: *the Right Rev. John P. Manley, Bishop of, etc.; the Bishop.*

Rigsdag (Danish parliament).

Rikers Island.

Riksdag (Swedish parliament).

rise. Do not use for increase in pay; use *raise* (which see).

riverfront.

Road. Spell out and capitalize in ordinary reading matter when part of a name: *Fordham Road.* The abbreviation (*Fordham Rd.*) may be used in headlines and in agate and other special matter.

roadbed.

Robert College (Turkey).

Rockefeller Center.

rocket age.

rock 'n' roll.

Rockville Centre (L.I.).

role.

roll-call.

roman. Do not capitalize if the reference is to letters, printing, types, etc. But capitalize *Roman* (and *Arabic*) numerals.

Roman Catholic Church. It is the Roman Catholic Church, not the Catholic Church. Also: a Roman Catholic. Use Roman in subsequent references also if the context does not make clear what is meant by Catholic. Do not capitalize *church* standing alone.

roommate.

Rosh ha-Shanah (Jewish New Year).

R.O.T.C. for Reserve Officers Training Corps.

round-. roundabout, round-bottomed, roundhouse, roundup (n.).
But: round robin (n.), round-robin (adj.).

route. Capitalize in names of roads: *Route 16.* The abbreviation may be used in headlines and special matter: *Rte. 16.*

rowboat.

Royal Mail Lines.

Royal Netherlands Steamship Company. For first references *a Royal Netherlands ship, etc.*, will suffice.

Royal Rotterdam Lloyd.

ruble.

rugby (football).

Rumania.

Rumanian Orthodox Episcopate of America.

run-. runaround (n.), rundown (adj.).

Russian names. Follow this system of transliteration for Russian names: Where there are English equivalents for letters in Russian use those equivalents. For other letters and symbols use phonetic renderings: *zh*, as in Zhukov; *kh*, as in Kharkov; *ts*, as in Trotsky; *ch*, as in Chernyshevsky; *sh*, as in Shostakovich; *shch*, as in the middle of Khrushchev; *ya*, as in Yalta.

Following is a complete transliteration table:

А а	a	У у	u
Б б	b	Ф ф	f
В в	v	Х х	kh
Г г	g	Ц ц	ts
Д д	d	Ч ч	ch
Е е	e[1]	Ш ш	sh
"	ye[2]	Щ щ	shch
"	yo[3]	ъ	—
Ж ж	zh	ы	y
З з	z	ь	—
И и	i	Э э	e
Й й	i	Ю ю	yu
К к	k	Я я	ya
Л л	l	**ADJECTIVAL**	
М м	m	**ENDINGS**	
Н н	n	ый	y
О о	o	ий	i
П п	p	ая	aya
Р р	r	яя	yaya
С с	s	ое	oye
Т т	t	ее	eye

[1]Use *e* after consonants.
[2]Use *ye* after vowels and after "soft sign," and in initial position.
[3]Use *yo* in certain special cases (see the following note).

There are two forms of *e* with three sounds: *ye*, as in Yevgeny; *yo*, as in Pyotr; *eh*, as in Edda. In written Russian, *ye* and *yo* look the same; only the pronunciation is different. Where we know the pronunciation is *yo*, we use it. Example: Semyon (spelled *Semen* in Russian). When in doubt, use *ye* or *e*.

Surnames that have the *ski* type of ending in Russian are spelled with *y* in English. Example: Malinovsky. Polish names take *i*. Example: Kolinski. Surnames with the *ov* type of ending are spelled with *v*, not *ff*. Example: Suvorov, not *Suvoroff*.

Women's names in Russian and some other languages have feminine endings. We do not use them unless a woman has an independent reputation under such a name. Example: Nina Petrovna Khrushchev, not *Khrushcheva*. Exception: Yekaterina Alekseyevna Furtseva, Soviet Minister of Culture and wife of Nikolai Firyubin.

Familiar names that have been rendered into English incorrectly should continue to be used in their familiar form. Examples: Peter the Great, not *Pyotr*; Khrushchev, not *Khrushchyov*; Rachmaninoff, not *Rakhmaninov*.

Emigré Russians decide how to spell their own names. Example: Nicholas Kalashnikoff, not *Nikolai Kalashnikov*.

Some names have been rendered incorrectly because they came into English through other languages. Be careful about taking Russian names from non-Russian sources. Whenever there is time, consult a Russian-speaking editor or reporter.

Russian Orthodox Greek Catholic Church of America.

Russians are only one of the many nationalities that make up the Soviet Union. *Russians* may be used in general references to citizens of the Soviet Union as a whole. But it should not be used when, for example, the reference is to Uzbeks or Latvians as such.

Russian wolfhound.

Rutland Railway.

S

Sabena, Belgian World Airlines. For first references *a Sabena airliner, etc.*, will suffice.

saber.

SAC for Strategic Air Command.

sacrilegious.

safe-. safe-conduct (n.), safe-cracker, safe-deposit (adj.), safeguard (n. and v.), safekeeping.

Sahara (not *Sahara Desert*).

sail-. sailboat, sailcloth, sailfish, sailmaker.

sailboats. For descriptions of the sailboat rigs now commonly used see **catboat, sloop, cutter, yawl, ketch, schooner.** Also see **yacht, yachting.**

sailing classes. Capitalize *Star Class, Lightning Class, etc.*

Saint John (N.B.), **St. Johns** (Que.), **St. John's** (Nfld.).

salable.

saloonkeeper.

Saltaire (L. I.).

Saluki (dog).

salvo, salvos.

Samoyed (dog).

Sands Point (L. I.).

Sanforized (trademark).

sang-froid.

sanitarium, sanitariums.

São Paulo (Brazil).

Sarajevo.

Sask. for Saskatchewan after cities and towns.

Satan. Also capitalize *Devil* if Satan is meant. Lower-case *a devil* and *devils*.

saturnalian.

savings and loan associations object to being called banks. A headline reference to such an association should begin with *Savings* or *Savings-Loan.* The irreducible minimum seems to be *Savings Agency.*

Saviour. This is the spelling when the reference is to Jesus or to God. Use *savior* for other meanings.

S. C. for South Carolina after cities and towns.

Scandinavian Airlines System, S.A.S.

Scarborough (N. Y.).

Schnauzer (dog).

school-. schoolbook, schoolboy, schoolchildren, schoolgirl, schoolhouse, schoolroom. But: school board, school ship.

school colors. Capitalize *Crimson, Blue, Red, etc.,* when referring to school colors and when designating teams by those colors.

school names. Do not use *No.* before numerical designations of public schools: *Public School 4, P.S. 4.* Capitalize full names: *Lincoln High School, Manley Junior High School.*

schooner. Now usually a two-masted yacht with the taller mast (main mast) stepped aft of the shorter mast (foremast). The rare schooner with more than two masts is designated as a three-masted (or four-, etc.) schooner.

scientific terms. See **chemical elements and formulas, genus and species.**

scores. See **sports.**

Scot (person), **Scottish** (adj.). **Scotch whisky.**

scotch plaid.

Scotch tape (trademark).

scot-free.

Scottish terrier.

screenplay.

Scripture(s). Capitalize in singular and plural when referring to books of the Old Testament and the New Testament. Lower-case *scriptural.* Set scriptural texts thus: *II Corinthians, iv, 3, etc.; seventh verse of the 53d Psalm; 53d chapter.*

scurrilous.

S. D. for South Dakota after cities and towns.

sea-. seacoast, seafarer, seagoer, seagoing, seaplane, seaport, seashore, seaweed. But: sea wall.

Seaboard Air Line Railroad.

Sealyham terrier.

Seaman John P. Manley (of the Navy), Seaman Manley, the seaman. Also: Seaman 2d Cl. John P. Manley, etc.

seasons. Do not capitalize *spring, summer, autumn, fall, winter.*

SEATO for Southeast Asia Treaty Organization.

S.E.C. for Securities and Exchange Commission.

Second Lieut. John P. Manley, Lieutenant Manley, the lieutenant.

Secretary, secretary. Secretary of Labor John P. Manley, Foreign Secretary, etc.; the Secretary. But: *John P. Manley, secretary of the company* (or *club, etc.*); *the secretary.*

Secretary General (of the United Nations) John P. Manley, the Secretary General.

secretary-treasurer. Hyphenate such coined compounds.

Security Council (United Nations), the Council.

securityholder.

self-. self-abasing, self-adulation, selfhood, self-made, selfness, self-respect, selfsame, self-service.

semi-. semiannual, semidarkness, semi-invalid, semiofficial, semiyearly.

semicolon. The semicolon is used principally as a mark of division in sentences containing statements that are closely related but require a separation more emphatic than a comma: *Peace is indivisible; if any*

European country is menaced, all are menaced. The contestants were ready; the timekeeper was not. The assignment was difficult; however, he carried it out.

The semicolon is also used in a series of three or more things that includes defining matter: *Those present were Thomas A. Jones, a banker; Robert G. Smith, a lawyer; Harold I. Abbot, a tax consultant, and John Trenton, a principal stockholder.*

If a semicolon and a closing quotation mark or a closing parenthesis appear together in a sentence, the semicolon should follow the other mark: *He said it was "bills, bills, bills"; she said it was his stinginess.*

In headlines, the semicolon is used only in tops or cross-lines to punctuate separate but related ideas. Do not use this mark in banks; the dash is used instead.

Seminola Park, Seminole Racing Park.

Senate. Capitalize all specific references, domestic and foreign.

Senator John P. Manley, Republican of Arizona; the Senator. Do not abbreviate, even in headlines.

Senator-elect John P. Manley, the Senator-elect.

senatorial.

send-off (n.).

senior (class and member of that class).

separate.

Sept. for September before numerals: *Sept. 17.*

septet. See **quartet** or **trio.**

sequence of tenses. In newspaper writing, the governing verb is generally in the past tense. For precision's sake, the tenses of other verbs in a sentence must be properly related to it. The following examples are offered as a guide.

He said he was sick. He was sick at the time he said so.

He pointed out that the earth is round. The *is* is right because the earth is always round.

He said he had been sick. He was sick at some time before the saying.

He said he was sick on July 4. Here a *had* is not needed to put the sickness back in time before the saying; *July 4* does that.

Jones is a sick man, Manley said, and cannot work. This means that Jones is sick now and Manley has so reported. The *said* is not the governing verb, but merely a parenthetical interpolation and thus *is* and *cannot* are correct. They would change to *was* and *could not* if the sentence read *Manley said that Jones, etc.*

Jones was a sick man, Manley said, and could not work. Here the meaning is that Jones was sick at some particular time in the past before Manley spoke.

Serbian Eastern Orthodox Church.

serenade. Capitalize in a title: *Beethoven's Serenade for Flute, Violin and Viola (Op. 25).* But: *a Mozart serenade.*

sergeant. See **Sgt.**

sergeant-at-arms.

sergeant first class. See **Sgt.**

sergeant major. See **Sgt.**

Sermon on the Mount.

serviceable.

serviceman.

set-. setback (n.), set-to (n.), setup (n.).

setter (dog).

Seventh-day Adventists.

Seventh Day Baptist General Conference.

Sèvres.

sextet. See **quartet** or **trio.**

Sgt. (or Sgt. 1st Cl., or Sgt. Maj.) John P. Manley, Sergeant Manley, the sergeant.

Shabuoth (Feast of Weeks).

Shakespearean.

shake-up (n.).

Shantung (cloth).

SHAPE for Supreme Headquarters Allied Powers (Europe).

shape-up (n.).

sheepdog.

sheik, sheikdom. See **Arab names.**

shell-shock.

Shepheard's Hotel (Cairo).

Sheriff John P. Manley, the sheriff.

Shetland (cloth and pony).

ship-. shipboard, shipbuilder, shipmate, shipowner, shipshape, shipyard.

ship lines are listed separately and alphabetically.

ship names. Do not quote them. Ships should be referred to as *she,* not *it,* even if the names are masculine.

shop-, -shop. shopkeeper, shoplifter, shopworn. Also: barbershop, bookshop, pawnshop, sweatshop, toyshop. But: machine shop, repair shop.

short (-). short circuit (n.), short-circuit (v.), short cut (n.), shorthand, shortsighted, shortstop.

shot-put, shot-putter, shot-putting.

show-. showboat, showdown, showman, show-off (n.), showroom.

shut-. shutdown (n.), shut-in (n.), shutout (n.).

S. I. for Staten Island after the names of communities.

sickroom.

side-. sidearm (style of pitching), sideboard, sideline, sidesaddle, side-step, side-stroke, sideswipe, sidewalk, sidewise. But: side arms (weapons).

sightsee, sightseeing, sightseer.

Signal Corps (United States), the corps.

signaled.

signatures should be set in caps and small caps: JOHN P. MANLEY. See **letters.**

simon-pure.

Sir John P. Manley, Sir John. In headlines: *Manley.*

sitdown (n.).

Six Nations. The Iroquois Confederacy.

sizable.

sizes. Express in numerals: *size 16 dress, size 44 long, 11½ B shoes, 16½ collar.*

skeptical.

ski, skied, skier, skiing.

skillful.

Skye terrier.

slang. The use of slang should be justified by the context. When it is used, avoid the self-conscious use of quotation marks.

sloop. A single-masted yacht that usually has one headsail (most often the jib). The mast is quite far forward. The distinction between sloop and cutter (which see) has almost disappeared.

slowdown (n.).

smallpox.

Smithsonian Institution.

smokescreen.

smolder.

smooth fox terrier.

snapshot.

sneak thief.

snow-. snowball, snow-blind, snowbound, snowfall, snowflake, snowplow, snowstorm.

so-called (adj.), **so called** (adv.).

Socialism. Capitalize if the reference is to a political party or movement that professes socialism. Lower-case in a general sense: *He told Congress that the plan smacked of socialism.*

Socialist. Capitalize as noun or adjective only if the reference is to a political party or movement that professes socialism, or to its members.

Society of Friends (Quakers).

solo, solos.

somber.

some-. somebody, someday (adv.), someone, sometimes (adv.).

sonata. Capitalize in a title: *Beethoven's "Moonlight" Sonata, Beethoven's Sonata in E flat, "Les Adieux."*

songs. Quote the titles of songs, popular or classical. If the title is in English, all the principal words are capitalized: *"Get Me to the Church on Time."* If the song is in French, Spanish, or Italian, the first word is generally capitalized: *"Nuit d'étoiles," "Il bacio."* If the song is in German, the first word and every noun are capitalized: *"An den Frühling."*

Soo Line Railroad.

sophomore (class and member of that class).

S O S (distress signal).

soundtrack.

soundtruck.

Southampton (L.I.).

South, south. Capitalize when referring to that geographic region of the United States; lower-case as a point of the compass.

South Asia comprises Afghanistan, Ceylon, India, Nepal and Pakistan.

Southeast Asia comprises Burma, Cambodia, Indonesia, Laos, Malaya, North Borneo, North Vietnam, South Vietnam, Sarawak and Thailand.

Southeast, southeast. Capitalize when referring to that geographic region of the United States; lower-case as a point of the compass.

Southern Baptist Convention.

Southern Pacific Company (railroad).

Southern Railway.

Southern, southern. Capitalize when used in reference to the South (geographic region) of the United States. But: *southern Utah, southern Italy, southern half, etc.*

Southerner. Capitalize when used to designate a native or inhabitant of the South (United States only).

South Jersey. An exception to the rule that calls for lower case in *southern New Jersey, southern Ohio, southern France, etc.* Also: *North Jersey.*

South Pole. But: *the pole, polar.*

South Shore (L. I.). Also: *North Shore.*

South Side. Capitalize when regularly used to designate a section of a city.

Southwest, southwest. Capitalize when referring to that geographic region of the United States; lower-case as a point of the compass.

Soviet, Soviets. *Soviet* and *Russia* may be used in headlines as synonyms for the Soviet Union. Do not use *Soviets,* in headlines or stories, as a synonym for the Soviet Union or its citizens. A soviet is a council. See **Russians.**

space-. spaceman, spaceship.

spaniel.

Spanish Line.

Spanish names usually contain the mother's family name, which comes after the father's family name. Thus, in a second reference to José Molina Valente, it is usually *Molina,* not *Valente.* However, some persons use both the mother's and the father's family names in second references.

SPAR for Coast Guard Women's Reserve, but *a Spar* for a member.

Speaker of the House. Always capitalized, unlike majority leader, minority leader, whip, etc., because it might otherwise not be recognized as a title. Also: *the Speaker.*

Specialist 4 (or 5, 6, etc.) John P. Manley, Specialist Manley, the specialist.

species. See **genus and species.**

specter.

speeches and lectures. Quote their full titles and capitalize principal words.

speed-. speedboat, speed-up (n.), speedway. But: speed trap.

spelling. The standard authorities for spelling in The New York Times are Webster's New International Dictionary, Second Edition, Unabridged, and the Columbia Lippincott Gazetteer of the World. For spelling of new words, particularly in the fields of science, Webster's Third New International Dictionary will be followed. Many troublesome words, especially compounds, are listed separately and alphabetically in the Style Book. The listed forms are to be used in cases of conflict with the dictionary or the gazetteer.

spilled (not *spilt*).

split infinitive. It should generally be avoided, but can sometimes be justified. For instance: *He was obliged to more than double the price.* But *to clearly show* should not have been split. A compound verb, however, should usually be separated when it is used with an adverb. See **adverb placement.**

split-up (n.).

sports. Scores and points are given in figures: *The Yankees won, 6 to 1. He scored 8 points in the first half. He shot a 4.* Numbers of runs, touchdowns, baskets, goals, strokes, etc., are spelled out below 10: *They had four hits and three runs in the eighth inning. In the 12th inning, they got their 11th hit, for a total of 10 runs. He took three more strokes.*

Times of sports events are expressed in figures: *3:01, 2:55½, 0.53.* When a time in seconds is given for the first time, it is set thus: *59.3 seconds.* In a subsequent reference, it is *0:59.3.* Also: *1 minute 3.2 seconds, 1:03.2.*

The names of sports events, stadiums, bowl games, etc. are capitalized but not quoted: *Kentucky Derby, Yankee Stadium, Rose Bowl Game, World Series, etc.*

Sports titles should precede a proper name only when the position is appointive or elective. *Coach Jack Manley, Manager Ralph Houk, Trainer Hirsch Jacobs.* But not *Outfielder Hank Aaron* or *Jockey Eddie Arcaro.*

See **automobile racing and rallies, baseball, basketball, boxing, cricket, football, hockey, horse racing, swimming, tennis, track and field, yachting.**

sportswear.

spring, springtime.

springer spaniel.

sputnik. Lower-case except in designations like *Sputnik V.*

Spuyten Duyvil.

squad (police). Lower-case *vice squad, loft squad,* etc.

Squadron Leader (British) John P. Manley, Squadron Leader Manley, the squadron leader.

Square. Spell out and capitalize in ordinary reading matter when part of a name: *Washington Square.* The abbreviation (*Washington Sq.*) may be used in headlines and in agate and other special matter.

Sr. for Senior in names. Do not use a comma: *John P. Manley Sr.* (or *Jr.*).

SS., St., Ste. for Saints, Saint, Sainte. The gazetteer is the guide for abbreviations in place names.

S. Sgt. John P. Manley, Sergeant Manley, the sergeant.

St. for Street. The abbreviation should be used only in headlines and special matter.

St. Andrew's (Westchester), **St. Andrews** (Scotland).

St. Bernard (dog).

St. Catharines (Ont.).

St. James's Palace, Court of St. James's.

St. Louis-San Francisco Railway, the Frisco.

St. Louis Southwestern Railway, the Cotton Belt.

stadiums. Capitalize the names of stadiums, playing fields, etc: *Yankee Stadium, Yale Bowl, Franklin Field, Madison Square Garden (the Garden).*

staff sergeant. See **S. Sgt.**

stagehand.

staid (sedate).

stanch is preferred to *staunch.*

stand-. stand-by (n.), stand-in (n.), standoff (n.), standpatter.

standard-bearer.

State, state. Capitalize *New York State* but not *state of Ohio, etc.,* unless reference is to a state's government. Lower-case references to specific states when standing alone: *The state sued the city. The state government acted.* Capitalize *State* when used with the name of an official agency or with an official title: *the State Education Department, State Controller John P. Manley.* Lower-case in the general sense: *affairs of state.*

state abbreviations. The abbreviations to be used for states of the United States when following the names of cities and towns are listed separately and alphabetically. Alaska, Hawaii, Idaho, Iowa, Ohio and Utah are not abbreviated.

State Assembly, the Assembly.

State Capitol, the Capitol.

state groupings. Capitalize designations like *New England States, Middle Atlantic States, Middle Western States, Southern States, Gulf Coast States, Mountain States, Pacific States, etc.,* when referring to the complete groupings.

State Senate, the Senate.

States Marine Lines.

states' rights.

statewide.

stationary (still), **stationery** (writing material).

steam-. steamboat, steamship, steam-fitter. But: steam engine.

step-. stepbrother, stepchild, stepfather.

stepping stone.

sterling. See **pounds, shillings and pence.**

stevedore. A stevedore, in waterfront usage, is an employer. A longshoreman is a laborer.

stiletto, stilettos.

stimulus, stimuli.

stock-. stockbroker, stockholder, stockjobber, stockman. But: stock room.

stock and commodity exchanges. The principal exchanges in the United States are listed separately and alphabetically.

Stock Yards (Chicago).

Stone Age.

stop-. stopgap, stoplight, stop-off (n.), stopover (n.).

store-, (-)store. storehouse, storekeeper, storeroom. Also: bookstore, cigar store, department store, drugstore, grocery store.

strait (passage) is almost always singular: Bering Strait, Strait of Gibraltar, Strait of Malacca. An exception is the Straits of Florida, although some authorities, but not The Times's, make that singular, too.

strait. straitjacket (n. and v.), straitlaced.

strangle. It means not merely to choke, but to choke to death. Also: strangle-hold.

stratum, strata.

streamline.

streetcar.

street-length (adj.).

streets and avenues. In giving the names of streets, avenues, etc., in ordinary reading matter, spell out and capitalize ordinal numerals through the ninth, *Avenue* and *Street, West, East,* etc.: *First Avenue, Fifth Avenue, Park Avenue, East Ninth Street.* Use figures for 10th and above: *10th Avenue, West 14th Street, 42d Street, West 113th Street.*

Avenue and *Street* may be abbreviated to *Ave.* and *St.* in headlines and in tabular or other special matter, but not in ordinary reading matter.

Give decades of streets in numerals: *the 20's, the 140's,* etc.

Use figures for all house numbers: *1 Fifth Avenue, 510 Broadway, 893 12th Avenue.* Do not use commas in numbers of more than three digits: *1135 11th Avenue.*

Do not use *No.* before a house number except in a sentence like this: *They rented 510 Broadway, but No. 512 remained vacant.*

Street numbers in Queens take a hyphen: *107-71 111th Street.*

In stories giving an avenue address in New York City, also give the nearest cross street.

strikebreaker.

strike-out (n.).

stroke oar.

strong-arm (v. and adj.).

stumbling block.

sub-. subbasement, subcommittee, subdivision, submachine gun, subnormal, subzero.

Subtreasury Building (in New York). It is now called the Federal Hall National Memorial, but Subtreasury Building may be used if the context warrants it.

Succoth (Feast of Tabernacles).

such. It is an adjective, not an adverb. *Such men are needed* is correct, but *such a high tax* is not. Make it *so high a tax.*

Sudan, the.

suffixes and prefixes. Words formed from them will be found under the separate and alphabetical listings of the suffixes and prefixes.

suffocate. Its most common meaning is not merely a stoppage of respiration, but a fatal stoppage.

suite (music). Capitalize in a title: *Bach's Suite No. 1 for Orchestra, Ravel's "Daphnis et Chloë" Suite No. 2.*

summer, summertime.

super-. superabundant, supercaution, supereloquent, superhighway, superindifference, supernatural. But: super-Republican.

Superintendent of Schools. John P. Manley, Superintendent of Schools; Superintendent Manley; the Superintendent.

supersede.

supra-. supra-auditory, suprafine, supragovernmental, supraintellectual, supranational.

Supreme Court (of the United States). Make it *the Court* in second references. The International Court of Justice (World Court) is the only other court to which this capitalization style applies. See **Chief Justice, Associate Justice.**

Surrogate John P. Manley, the surrogate.

Swedish American Line.

swimming. Times of races are given in figures: *57.6 seconds, 0:57.6.* The order of finish in a swimming race is determined by the judges, not the timers.

The pool length should be carried in all stories. World records can be set only in pools that are 50 meters or 55 yards long. American records can be set in three categories, according to pool length: 20 yards, 25 yards (known as short course) and 50 meters or 55 yards (known as long course).

Swissair.

symphony. A symphony without a nickname or a special title is capitalized but not quoted: *Brahms's Symphony No. 1, or Brahms's First Symphony.* A nickname is quoted: *Beethoven's "Eroica" Symphony.* The whole of a special title is quoted: *"Symphonie Fantastique."* Capitalize the name of a movement: *the Scherzo, the Andante.* Lowercase if the movement is referred to by its place in the sequence: *the third movement, the finale.* If the

opus number is cited, it should be within parentheses: *Tchaikovsky's Symphony No. 4 in F minor (Op. 36).* If it is a Mozart symphony, the Köchel catalogue number should be used within parentheses: *Mozart's Symphony No. 40 in G minor (K. 550).*

syllabus, syllabuses.

Synagogue Council of America. Congregational and rabbinical groups of the three branches of Judaism — Orthodox, Reform and Conservative — are represented on the council.

Synod. Capitalize in the name of a church organization.

Syrian Antiochian Orthodox Church.

Syrian (Orthodox) Church of Antioch.

T

Tabasco (trademark).

tableau, tableaus.

table d'hôte.

tablespoonful(s).

taboo.

tailor-made.

Taiwan (not *Formosa*).

take-off (n., adj.).

TB for tuberculosis.

tea-. tearoom, teaspoonful(s), teatime.

team-. teammate, team play, teamwork.

teamsters. See **International Brotherhood of Teamsters.**

technical sergeant. See **T. Sgt.**

Technicolor (trademark).

teen-age, teen-ager. Do not use *teen* by itself.

Teleprompter (trademark).

Teletype, Teletypesetter (trademarks).

telltale.

temperature. Use figures for degrees of temperature: *The temperature was 9 at midnight. Heat of 92.5 degrees was reported. There was a 40-degree drop during the night. His temperature was 101.9.* Do not write, *He had a temperature.* Either *He had a high temperature* or *He had a fever.* The degree mark is available for use in headlines and tabular matter: *60°.* In stories, spell out an indefinite number: *The temperature stayed in the nineties for three hours.* In headlines, *90's* may be used.

tempos (not tempi).

Ten Commandments (Decalogue). Do not abbreviate or use figures: *First Commandment.* Also *Tenth Commandment* (an exception to the style of using figures for ordinals above the ninth).

Tenn. for Tennessee after cities and towns.

tennis. Use figures in scores: *30—15, 30—all, 40—love.* Use *scores* instead of *score* in referring to the result of a match of more than one set: *The scores of the match were 6—1, 3—6, 9—7.*

Players hitting the ball back and forth are rallying, not volleying. A player volleys when he hits the ball before it strikes the ground.

terrier.

terror-. terror-ridden, terror-stricken, terror-struck.

testimony. Set testimony full measure and do not use quotation marks. Make the question and the answer one paragraph unless they are so long that they would be typographically unattractive if combined. Use Q. and A. except where the questioner and the person questioned are identified for the first time. In most cases, of course, the introduction to the Q. and A. matter will supply such information. Use no dash after Q. or A.

tête-à-tête.

Tex. for Texas after cities and towns.

texts. Texts are set in the regular 8-point body type of The Times. In general, texts up to seven columns in length are indented; those longer than seven columns are set full measure. The introductions to texts are set one-column 8-point italic full measure or two-column 9-point italic full measure. Texts and textual excerpts presented in textual form are not quoted. The typographical treatment of texts is discussed in more detail in the supplement.

Thai (person and adj.).

Thanksgiving, Thanksgiving Day.

that, which. *That* is preferred in restrictive clauses: *The university that he admires most is Harvard.* In nonrestrictive clauses, *which* is mandatory: *Harvard, which is not his alma mater, is first in his affections.*

the. Capitalize when an integral part of a name: *The Hague, The New York Times.* But: *the Netherlands.* See **a, an** and **articles**.

theater, theatergoer. Capitalize *Theater* in names: *the Shubert Theater.*

The Dalles (Ore.).

The Hague.

Thermos (trademark). The general term is *vacuum bottle.*

thoroughgoing.

thrash (to beat a person), **thresh** (to harvest grain). Also: *thresh out a problem.*

Throgs Neck.

Thruway.

thunder-. thunderbolt, thunderclap, thundercloud, thunderhead, thunderstorm.

tidelands. The area between the high-tide and low-tide marks. See **offshore oil.**

tidewater.

tie-up (n.).

tightrope.

tilde. See **accent marks.**

time. Use numerals in giving clock time: *10:30 A.M.* (the preferred form because it is the shortest), *10:30 o'clock, 10:30.* Do not use *half-past 10.* Also avoid the redundant *10:30 A.M. yesterday morning, Monday afternoon at 2 P.M.*

    The times in the time zones of the United States are: Eastern standard (or daylight) time (E.S.T., E.D.T.), central standard time (C.S.T.), mountain standard time (M.S.T.), Pacific standard time (P.S.T.). Include when pertinent to the story: *10 A.M. yesterday, central standard time.* Also: summer time, Greenwich mean time (G.M.T.).

    In giving elapsed times of voyages, races, etc., do not use commas: *4 days 16 hours 13 minutes.*

    See **days, weeks, months, years, centuries** and **sports.**

Time & Life Building.

titleholder.

titles. Personal titles of all sorts—academic, business, foreign, governmental, military, religious, etc.—are listed separately and alphabetically, and the style for capitalization or abbreviation is given in each case. Long titles should follow names: *John P. Manley, Minister of Internal Affairs.*

    In the titles of books, plays, speeches, etc., the principal words should be capitalized: *"The Catcher in the Rye," The World Almanac, "A Taste of Honey," "American Prospects and Foreign Trade,"* etc. Separate and alphabetical listings of the categories of titles show whether quotation marks are to be used or not.

TNT.

toastmaster.

tobacco, tobaccos.

to-do (n.).

toll bridge.

Toms River (N.J.).

tongue-tied

ton-miles.

top-. topcoat, topgallant, top-heavy, topknot, topmast, topsail.
    But: top hat.

topsy-turvy.

Tory, Tories.

totaled, totaling.

touch-. touch-and-go (adj.),
touchback, touchdown, touchhole,
touch-me-not (n.).

towboat.

track and field. Times of races are
given in figures: *9.3 seconds, 0:09.3,
3 minutes 58.6 seconds, 3:58.6.*

Spell out mile distances up to 10:
*one-mile walk, two-mile run, 10-
mile run.* Use figures for all races
measured in yards and meters: *60-
yard dash, 100-yard dash, 200-meter
dash.*

Figures are also used in field
events to show height and distance.
A pole vaulter clears 15 feet 4 inches.
The next reference to the height
should be to 15—4 (eliminating feet
and inches).

A shot is *put*, not thrown or
heaved. The shot is the iron ball, the
put the body motion used to propel
it.

trademarks. Names of products and
processes that are patented and are
the exclusive property of an individual or company are capitalized:
Coca-Cola (and *Coke*), *Frigidaire,
Kodak, Technicolor, Thermos, Victrola, etc.* These and others are listed
separately and alphabetically. The
use of trademarks can easily be
avoided if desirable: *bandage* for
Band-Aid, vacuum bottle for *Thermos, etc.* But if a trade name is per-
tinent to a story, use it: *The robbers
escaped in a 1961 Cadillac sedan.*

train-miles.

trans-. trans-Atlantic,
transcontinental, transmigrate,
transoceanic, trans-Pacific,

transship, transshipment,
trans-Siberian.

Trans-Canada Air Lines.

Trans World Airlines.

traveled, traveler, traveling.

treaties, pacts and plans. Capitalize
specific names: *Treaty of Ghent,
Treaty of Versailles, Versailles
Treaty, Pact of Paris.* But: *nine-
power treaty, United States-Cana-
dian trade treaty.* Capitalize *Alliance for Progress, Truman Doctrine,
Marshall Plan* and similar designations that have acquired official or
semiofficial stature.

tri-. triangular, tricentennial,
tricolor, trilateral, trilingual,
trimonthly, tripartite, tristate,
triweekly.

Triborough Bridge.

trio. Capitalize in the title of a musical work: *Mozart's Piano Trio in
B flat major (K. 254), Beethoven's
"Archduke" Trio.* Capitalize in the
name of an ensemble: *Vienna Trio.*

trophies (sports). Capitalize *America's Cup, Davis Cup,* etc.

tryout (n.).

T. Sgt. John P. Manley, Sergeant Manley, the sergeant.

tugboat.

turboprop may be used, as adjective
or noun, in reference to a plane with
propellers driven by jet engines. Do
not use *turbojet* in this sense; it is
a type of engine. See **jet, jetliner.**

turn-. turncoat, turndown (n.),
turnkey (n.), turnover (n.),
turnout (n.).

TV for television.

T.V.A. for Tennessee Valley Authority.

tying.

tyro, tyros.

Tyrol (not *the Tyrol*).

U

U.A.W. for United Automobile Workers (which see).

Ukraine, the.

Ukrainian Orthodox Church of America.

ukulele.

ultra-. ultra-atomic, ultra-German, ultramodern, ultranationalism, ultraviolet.

umlaut. See **accent marks.**

un-. unaffected, un-American, unbiased, undo, unforgettable, unsolved.

U.N. for United Nations, but only in headlines, quoted matter or tabular or other special matter.

under-. underbid, underclerk, underclothes, underconsumption, underdeveloped, underdog, underdone, underestimate, undergraduate, underground, underhand, underripe, undersheriff, understudy, underworld, underwrite. But: under secretary (which see), under way (adv.).

Under Secretary of State John P. Manley, the Under Secretary.

UNESCO for United Nations Educational, Scientific and Cultural Organization.

UNICEF for United Nations Children's Fund, even though *International* and *Emergency* have been dropped from the name.

Uniform Code of Military Justice.

Union-Castle Line (Union-Castle Mail Steamship Company, Ltd.)

Union of American Hebrew Congregations. A Reform group.

Union of Orthodox Jewish Congregations.

Union of Orthodox Rabbis.

Union of Soviet Socialist Republics (U.S.S.R.).

Union Pacific Railroad.

unique. A dangerous word that should be avoided.

Unitarian Universalist Association.

United Air Lines.

United Automobile Workers may be used in first references instead of the full name, the United Automobile, Aircraft and Agricultural Implement Workers of America. The abbreviation is U.A.W.

United Church of Christ. A merger of the Evangelical and Reformed Church and the Congregational Christian Churches.

United Nations Charter, the Charter.

United Nations Economic and Social Council, the Council. Note that this is not UNESCO.

United Nations General Assembly, the Assembly.

United Nations Secretariat, the Secretariat.

United Nations Security Council, the Council.

United Nations Trusteeship Council, the Council.

United Presbyterian Church in the U. S. A.

United Press International. Use without an article in references in stories. U.P.I. is the abbreviation, but the periods are not used in datelines: LIEGE, Belgium, May 3 (UPI)—etc. Use agate credit line above the dateline on Page 1 stories:

By United Press International

United States. Do not abbreviate in stories, except in names, designations of highways and quoted matter.

United States Air Force, the Air Force. But lower-case *air force* in subsequent references to a foreign air force.

United States Army, the Army. But lower-case *army* in subsequent references to a foreign army.

United States Lines.

United States Marine Corps, the Marine Corps, the Marines (meaning the corps). But: *three marines, a company of marines.*

United States Navy, the Navy. But lower-case *navy* in subsequent references to a foreign navy.

United Synagogue of America. A Conservative group.

Unity of the Brethren.

unprecedented. A dangerous word that should be avoided.

up-, -up. upgrade, uphill, upstairs, upstate, uptown, up-to-date (adj.). Also (all n.): build-up, close-up, crack-up, frame-up, grownup, holdup, line-up, make-up, mix-up, pushup, setup, shake-up, shape-up, speed-up, tie-up, walk-up, windup.

U.S. for United States, but only in headlines, names, quoted matter or tabular and other special matter. Use the abbreviation in road names: *U.S. 40.*

U.S.I.A. for United States Information Agency.

U.S.I.S. for United States Information Service. It is used to designate branches of the U.S.I.A.

U.S.S. for a United States ship in Government service. Where it is appropriate in stories make it *the U.S.S. Saratoga,* but *the aircraft carrier Saratoga* is usually better. Use U.S.S. in datelines: ABOARD U.S.S. SARATOGA, at Sea (or some other locating phrase), May 10—etc.

U.S.S.R. for Union of Soviet Socialist Republics after cities and towns.

Utah. Do not abbreviate after cities and towns.

utopian.

V

Va. for Virginia after cities and towns.

V.A. for Veterans Administration.

Valley. Capitalize when part of a name: *Mississippi Valley.* But: *the valley.*

Van Cortlandt Park.

variations (music). Capitalize in a title: *Brahms's Variations on a Theme by Haydn.*

varicolored.

Varig Airlines.

Vaseline (trademark).

V. D. for veneral disease.

vender.

verse set in verse style does not require quotation marks. Normally verse should be set in 6½-point type.

versus. Use *vs.* in news and sports matter, and *v.* in court cases and proceedings of the United States Supreme Court.

Very Rev. John P. Manley, the; Dean of, Provincial of, etc.

vet. Do not use for veteran except in AMVETS.

Veterans Day. Nov. 11, formerly Armistice Day.

vicar. Lower-case except when part of a title: *Vicar of Christ* (the Pope), *Vicar of Wakefield, etc.*

Vice Adm. John P. Manley, Admiral Manley, the admiral.

Vice Consul John P. Manley, Vice Consul Manley, the vice consul.

vice-consulate.

Vice President John P. Manley, Vice President Manley, the Vice President (of a national government only), the vice president (of a subdivision of a national government, a company, club, etc.).

Vice-Presidential, Vice-Presidency. Capitalize where the reference is to the office of Vice President of the United States.

Vice President-elect John P. Manley, Vice President-elect Manley, the Vice President-elect (of a national government; otherwise, lower case).

vice versa.

vichyssoise.

victoria (carriage).

Victrola (trademark).

Vietminh.

Vietnam, Vietnamese (person and adj.).

Vietnamese names. In general, follow the Vietnamese practice of using full names in second as well as in first references: Ngo Dinh Diem, not *Ngo* (the family name) or *Diem*. But an exception is made in the case of President Ngo Dinh Diem to permit the use of *Diem* alone in headlines.

vilify.

Village. Capitalize when used alone to mean Greenwich Village. Do not quote, except in headlines.

Virgin Mary, the Virgin.

virtuoso, virtuosos.

visa, visaed.

vis-à-vis.

Viscount Astor, Lord Astor, the viscount.

Viscountess Astor, Lady Astor, the viscountess.

vitamin A (or *B, G, etc.*).

Voice of America. Capitalize and do not quote, except "Voice" alone and then only if necessary to avoid confusion.

voilà.

voodoo.

votes. Use figures in giving the results of voting: *The vote was 51 to*

3, with 3 abstentions. A majority of 9 was obtained. He received 6 votes. Of these, 4 were invalid.

voting districts. See **district.**

Vt. for Vermont after towns.

vying.

W

Wabash Railroad.

WAC for Women's Army Corps. But *a Wac* for a member.

WAF for Women in the Air Force, but *a Waf* for a member.

wage-earner.

Wailing Wall (Jerusalem).

waistline.

walk-. walk-on (n.), walkout (n.), walkover (n.), walk-up (n.).

wallpaper.

war-. warlike, warpath, warship, wartime.

Wards Island.

ware-. warehouse, warehouseman, wareroom.

Warrant Officer John P. Manley, Mr. (or Warrant Officer) Manley, the warrant officer.

wash-. washbowl, washout (n.), washroom.

Wash. for Washington after cities and towns.

Washington's Birthday (holiday).

water-. water-color, waterfall, waterfront, waterline, waterlogged, waterproof, watershed, waterway, waterworks.

water spaniel.

wave length.

WAVES for Women Accepted for Volunteer Emergency Service. But *a Wave* for a member.

W.C.T.U. for Women's Christian Temperance Union.

week-. weekday, weekend, week-long.

weeks. Capitalize officially designated weeks: *Apple Week, Music Week, etc.*

weird.

well-. well-being, well-bred, well-founded, well-groomed, well-known, well-timed, well-to-do, well-wisher.

West, west. Capitalize when referring to that geographic region of the United States and to the grouping of nations opposed to the Communists in the ideological division of the world. Lower-case as a point of the compass.

Westchester (N. Y.), **West Chester** (Del., Pa.).

West Coast, west coast. Capitalize when referring to the region of the United States lying along the shoreline of the Pacific; lower-case when referring to the actual shoreline. Also: *the Coast* (but capitalize for West Coast only).

West End (London).

Western Airlines.

Western Front (battlefront).

Western Maryland Railway.

Western Pacific Railroad.

Western, western. Capitalize when referring to the geographic region of the United States and to the grouping of nations opposed to the Communists in the ideological division of the world. But: *western Ohio, western Hungary, western half, etc.*

Westerner. Capitalize when used to designate a native or inhabitant of the West (United States only).

Westhampton (L. I.).

West Highland white terrier.

West Side. Capitalize when regularly used to designate a section of a city. Note: In London it is West End.

whereabouts (sing.).

which, that. See that, which.

whip (legislative title). Lower-case: *John P. Manley, the Republican whip in the House.*

whippet (small hound).

whisky, whiskies.

white-. whitecap, white-headed, whitewing.

white paper. Lower-case unless it is part of a name: *The State Department issued a white paper on China.*

W.H.O. for World Health Organization.

wholehearted.

wide-, -wide. wide-awake, wide-brimmed, wide-eyed. widesought. Also: citywide, countrywide, nationwide, statewide, worldwide.

Wilkes-Barre (Pa.).

wilton carpet.

wind-. windfall, windmill, windstorm.

windup (n.).

Wing Comdr. (British) John P. Manley, Wing Commander Manley, the wing commander.

winter, wintertime.

wire fox terrier (not *wire-haired*).

wiretapping.

Wis. for Wisconsin after cities and towns.

woebegone.

Woodbridge, Wood-Ridge, (N. J.).

Woods Hole (Mass.).

woodwork.

Wool Associates of the New York Cotton Exchange.

woolen, woolly.

work-. workaday, workday, workhouse, workout (n.), workman (or workingman), workshop.

World Bank may be used instead of International Bank for Reconstruction and Development (the official name) in second references and in first references if necessary to avoid a cumbersome sentence.

World Court may be used instead of International Court of Justice (the official name) in second references. Also: *the Court.*

World Series. Capitalize when referring to the baseball series between the American and National Leagues. Also: *Little World Series* (baseball).

World War I, World War II. *First World War* and *Second World War* may also be used, but the Roman-numeral form is preferred.

worldwide.

worshiper, worshiping, worshiped.

worthwhile (n., adj.).

wrongdoer.

W. Va. for West Virginia after cities and towns.

Wyo. for Wyoming after cities and towns.

X

Xmas. Never use.

X-ray (n., adj., v.).

Y

yacht. A sailboat or a powerboat, usually privately owned, that is used for the pleasure of racing or cruising. See the following entry and **sailboats.**

yachting. Times of yacht and boat races are given in figures: *4 hours 10 minutes 23 seconds, 4:10:23; 10 minutes 54 seconds, 10:54.* In yacht races, when the time of the race and the hour of the day are given, follow this form: *The Puritan started at 9:30 and reached the stake boat at 2:15:20* (meaning at 15 minutes 20 seconds past 2 o'clock). *She won the race in 4:45:20* (meaning in 4 hours 45 minutes 20 seconds), *beating the Priscilla by 6 minutes and the Genesta by 9 minutes 15 seconds.*

When possible, stories should carry the direction and speed of the wind. Speed is shown in miles an hour or in knots, not knots *an hour.*

Most competition in the metropolitan area is conducted among one-design classes. These classes are referred to as the *Star Class, Thistle Class, etc.* (dropping the *one-design*). Exception: *Manhasset Bay One-Design Class.* Figures are used for metric designations: 5.5-Meter yacht, 12-Meter yacht.

In predicted log contests for both sailboats and powerboats, the skipper predicts in writing how long it will take him to cover a given course. His score is based on how close he comes to his estimate. Such events should not be referred to as races.

yard-, -yard. yardarm, yardmaster, yardstick. Also: backyard, barnyard, churchyard, graveyard, lumberyard, schoolyard, steelyard, studdingsail-yard.

yawl. A two-masted vessel in which the mizzen (the small mast aft) is stepped aft of the yacht's waterline. See **ketch.**

years. Numerals are almost always used to designate specific years: *1492, 1961.* Decades of years may be spelled out (the preferred form in stories) or given in figures: *the nineteen-thirties, the 1930's.* When the century is omitted in stories, the decade is spelled out and lowercased: *the thirties.* But special designations like *the Roaring Twenties* should be capitalized. In headlines, a single year may be given as *'60,* a decade as *60's.*

Spans of years are given as follows: *1861-65, 1880-95, 1895-1900, 1903-4* (not *1903-04*).

Spell out numbers of centuries from first through ninth and lowercase: *the first century, the eighth century.* Use numerals from 10th on: *the 12th century, the 19th century.* Hyphenate the adjectival form: *eighth-century ruins, 17th-century house.*

Yeoman John P. Manley, Yeoman Manley, the yeoman. Also: Yeoman 3d Cl. John P. Manley, etc.

yogurt.

Yoknapatawpha County.

Yom Kippur (Day of Atonement).

Yorkshire terrier.

Your Honor. Capitalize when referring to the judge or other presiding officer in a court, but use only in quoted matter.

Yule, Yuletide. Yule is overworked in headlines and should be the last resort.

Yugoslav (person and adj.).

Z

zabaglione.

zero, zeros.

zigzag (adj., n., v.).

Zim Lines (Zim Israel Navigation Company, Ltd.).

zip gun. Do not quote or hyphenate: *John P. Manley, whose many accomplishments include the invention of the zip gun, has retired to write his memoirs.*

Supplement

Proofreader's Marks

⊙ Period.

, Comma.

= Hyphen.

: Colon.

; Semicolon.

Apostrophe.

Quotations.

□ Indent one em; doubled for two ems, and so on.

One em dash; change figure for longer dash.

Push down lead or space.

Close up.

Less space.

∧ Caret—something to be inserted.

Turn—letter, line or matter.

Insert space.

tr. Transpose—letters, lines or matter.

Character to go around letters, words, phrases, sentences or paragraphs to indicate that they are to be transposed, always to be accompanied by the mark "tr," on the margin of the proof.

stet. Let it stand—this when something has been inadvertently crossed out; dots placed under the matter will usually suffice, but the term "stet" will better avoid misunderstanding.

Delete—take out.

X Broken letter or bad type.

Paragraph; with "no" preceding it when no paragraph is intended.

w.f. Wrong font—letter or character belonging to another face.

Equalize spacing.

cap Capitalize word or words—in copy indicated by three under-strokes.

sm.c Small capitals—indicated by two under-strokes.

l.c. Lower-case—reduce from a capital to a small letter.

Superior characters—for footnotes, in horse racing tables, etc.

Inferior figures—used in chemical formulas, mathematical problems, etc.

ital. Italic type—indicated in copy by underscoring the word or words to be italicized.

rom. Roman—from italic or full-face.

⊐ or ⊏ Set out to margin indicated.

⊓ or ⊔ Move up or down.

( ) Parentheses.

[ ] Brackets.

spell Spell out, if figures.

◯ A circle around figures in copy means spell out; if around a word, set in figures.

(Most of these marks are also applicable to manuscript)

SPEED ON THE RAILS

Streamlined Schedules That Cover the Country

Last week a *silvery streak* of stainless steel sped out of Los Angeles, climbed swiftly over Arizona Rockies, up the old Santa Fe Trail and across Kansas, taking in a corner of the dust bowl, and hit Chicago for a new rail record between the two cities—2,228 miles at more than a mile a minute. This was the latest recruit to join the parade of fast, luxurious streamlined trains that have been making railroad history the last few years

Today, particularly in the West, there is scarcely a single run between important cities that does not have its special fast train maintaining a remarkable time schedule and offering passengers the last word in interior equipment as well as unusual beauty of line in exterior appearance.

How Speed Is Made

The speeding up of trains on specials runs in recent years is in itself an epic in railroading. Five years ago there were hardly more than a handful that ran long distances at 60 miles an hour or more. A year ago there were more than 400, and today about 650 hold to that schedule and the number is constantly increasing

The increased speed has been attained by varied methods. Streamlining itself helps at more than fifty miles per hour. Many of the trains are of lightweight construction, weighing about half as much as the older type, and this, engineers claim, permits greater speed without corresponding increases in fuel cost or in track and equipment maintenance.

More than 100 high speed locomotives, costing about $15,000,000, have been put into service since the first of the year. Huge Diesel-electric engines, streamlined and artistically decorated in the same leitmotiv as the cars they pull, race over prairies and tablelands

Make-up Markers

Changes in stories and headlines already in type are to be indicated as follows:

Special to The New York Times.

UNITED NATIONS, N. Y., May 1—Britain warned today that she might withdraw her cooperation if the United Nations Committee of Seventeen on colonialism permitted itself to be "stampeded by propaganda and vituperation."

Kill for new lead Dean

The strongly worded statement was made by Sir Patrick Dean, chief of the British delegation to the United Nations. Although he did not mention the Soviet Union, it was clear that he was alluding to a Soviet resolution on Northern Rhodesia put before the committee last week.

The resolution criticized the British territory's new Constitution as "racialist and 'antidemocratic" and called for independence no later than Dec. 31.

Turn rule for Insert A Dean

A subcommittee on Southern Rhodesia made public yesterday a report that said there had been no concrete results from talks in London earlier this month between the subcommittee's members and high-ranking British officials. The report warned of impending violence in Southern Rhodesia if the rights of Africans there were not substantially increased.

Kill for Insert B Dean

The tone of Sir Patrick's address was believed to reflect increasing British concern over both Rhodesias, which, together with Nyasaland, make up the Federation of Rhodesia and Nyasaland. Britain is attempting to mediate between the white settlers of the Federation, led by its Prime Minister, Sir Roy Welensky, and the increasingly nationalist and numerically dominant African population.

Turn rule for add at end Dean

White Plains Tax Rise Due

Special to The New York Times.

WHITE PLAINS, May 1— City officials here reported today that the municipal tax rate for the year beginning July 1 would rise to $32 for each $1,000 of assessed valuation, an increase of $1.80. The additional rate for schools currently is for the next fiscal year.

Must kill for sub

Swede to Teach at Princeton

Special to The New York Times.

PRINCETON, N. J., May 1— Dr. Lennart Uhlin, a member of the faculty of the Swedish Royal Institute of Technology at Stockholm, will be a visiting professor in Princeton University's School of Architecture during the fall term.

Must kill— dupe

SCHOOL STAY WON BY NEW ORLEANS

Desegregation Plan Delayed by New U. S. Judge

Kill for sub C head Orleans— story stands

Park Preservation Will Be Promoted With Lapel Buttons

Kill for sub 3=X head Parks—with sub story

Typography of Texts

Following are some general guides to the typographical treatment of textual matter. They are intended to improve the appearance of our texts and to introduce uniformity of handling. Since texts tend to defy a common mold, the principles here put down may not cover every case. Still, incomplete though it may be, the code should serve to point the way to what is desired in general and should provide a guide when improvisation is necessary.

How to approach a text

First: Leaf through it to establish which headings and subheadings are coordinate and which should receive emphasis.

Second: Notice how many gradations of headings there are. These will establish how many variations of type will be required.

Third: Examine the lengths of the headings. These will have a bearing on the selection of type.

Fourth: Observe any tabulations or listings that may require special treatment.

Fifth: Consider whether the text would be clarified by illustration—maps, charts, photographs. If the text runs two columns or more some kind of illustration is desirable for appearance's sake, even if it is not necessary for clarification.

Type for headings

1. To enhance the appearance of the paper we should keep to a minimum the diversity of type faces. In selecting type for headings in texts this cause can be served by confining ourselves by and large to Ideal (our body type) when 6½ pt.,

8 pt. and 9 pt. are desired and to Century (which is substantially the same) when sizes above 9 pt. are desired.

2. In any type face the capital letters occupy almost the entire body and the lower case letters only a half to two-thirds of the entire body. Thus, whereas a line of 10 pt. set entirely in caps will be virtually 10 points high, a line of 10 pt. set in caps and lower case (with the small letters normally greatly outnumbering the capitals) will give the appearance of being only 5 or 7 points high. For example:

THESE 10 PT. CHARACTERS ARE VIRTUALLY 10 PTS. HIGH
But Most of These Are Considerably Smaller

Two conclusions are to be drawn from this:

(a) If, for instance, the general run of headings in a text are to be set in 10 pt. caps and lower case and it is desired to give a greater prominence to a few more important headings, it is not advisable to use both caps *and* a larger size; this will give too great a difference in weight. The major headings might be set either in 10 pt. caps or in 12 pt. caps and lower case. (See also Paragraph 10.)

(b) A larger point size will not invariably give a line greater prominence than the next smaller size; it depends on whether the line is set in caps or in caps and lower case. For example, a line of 10 pt. caps will be as prominent as a line of 12 pt. caps and lower case. Thus:

THIS IS 10 PT. CENTURY BOLD CAPS
This Is 12 Pt. Cent. Bold u. & l. c.

3. For headings of single-column width the maximum sizes should be: if all caps—12 pt.; if caps and lower case—14 pt.

4. Headings that are part of the text should never look like our own subheads; that is, a textual heading that is a single line centered should never be set in 8 pt. fflc.

5. If each of the textual headings will fit into a single line

they may be set in 10 pt. Century bold caps and lower case centered; in a long text 12 pt. may be better.

10 pt. Century Bold u. & l. c.

General Principles

12 pt. Century Bold u. & l. c.

General Principles

6. If some or all of the textual headings will run over into two lines they may all be set in 10 pt. or 12 pt. Century bold caps and lower case *flush left* within indent. When they appear under other headings that are centered it is preferable to set them inverted pyramid style instead of flush left.

This Is 10 Pt. Cent. Bold u. & l. c. Fl. Left Within Indent	BUT IN THIS CASE Since These Follow a Centered Line They Are Pyramided

7. If some or all of the textual subheadings will run into three or more lines they may be set 9 pt. fflc flush and one within indent, thus:

IV. The Obstacles Which Frustrated the Efforts of His Majesty's Government to Establish Self-Governing Institutions in Palestine.

or, if they are not excessively long, 8 pt. ff caps flush and one within indent, thus:

IV. THE OBSTACLES TO ESTABLISHING SELF-GOVERNING INSTITUTIONS.

8. In printing documents it is desirable, wherever possible, not to use our own subheads to break up the text. Sometimes the textual headings themselves will be sufficient. Sometimes if there are numbered paragraphs the numbers may be centered and bracketed in boldface and they will serve to break up long sections of type. (If, however, there are lettered or

numbered subdivisions under the main numbers these letters or numbers should not be centered, but rather retained at the beginnings of the paragraphs.) An example of this treatment:

[1]

If this were an official document this paragraph might start with the figure 1. The editor, in marking it for the composing room, would use the figure 1 to break up the text, centering it at the head of the paragraph and striking it out at the start of the paragraph.

[2]

(a) Should any of the paragraphs so numbered be subdivided, however, as are this and the following one, the editor would not center the letter or symbol designating the subdivision but would have it set as it is here.

(b) This paragraph is thrown in here merely to show that where there is an (a) there should be a (b).

9. Cheltenham may be used in some cases for our own headings, as contrasted with those of the text itself; for example, if we are printing two diplomatic notes, the headings "The British Note" and "The Soviet Reply" may be set in Cheltenham. In these cases use Chelt. bold condensed caps and lower case in either 12 pt. (the P head) or 14 pt., depending on the length of the text.

P Head

U. S. Proposal

There is given below a brief general statement of the type of treaty envisioned by the United States Government as proper.

Soviet Note

On Oct. 26 of this year, during his conversation with J. A. Malik, Mr. Dulles pre-

10. If headings are to appear one under another, contrast should be sought. Instead of using merely different sizes of caps and lower case, the editor can obtain contrast by alter-

nating caps and lower case with all caps or, if additional variations are required, by using italics and caps and small caps, but it should be noted that only 10 per cent of the machines in the composing room are equipped with italics and caps and small caps. Therefore, these should be used sparingly. For example:

GENERAL PRINCIPLES
Chapter I
PURPOSES OF THE ARMED FORCES
Article 1

or

PART III
ANNEX TO THE
SUGGESTIONS
Territorial Matters.

11. Aside from listings or tabular matter, G caps are best avoided. Regular light caps or caps and small caps will usually serve the same purpose more attractively.

12. A lengthy text can be effectively dressed by setting the major headings 2-column measure. The type in this case would be 12 pt. Century Bold caps and lower case, although if there are two or three different lines in the headings, lines of all caps and lines of italic caps and lower case may also be used for contrast. Since 2-column headings create make-up problems they should be used only in texts that are in the composing room early in the evening. Another caution: If in one or more cases the body matter under a major heading is very brief and would not provide enough type to be doubled up attractively, it is not advisable to use 2-column headings. A few samples:

12 pt. Cent. Bold 2-col. measure

Organization of the Mission

Greek physical assets, such as transportation facilities, com- | Greece, under Export-Import Bank loans, or obtained under

CHAPTER I

Historical Introduction

The sixteen participating countries with Western Germany have a total population | A high level of agricultural production was attained, based in some cases on the special-

CHAPTER V
Recommendations

The line "Introductory Statement" is set in 9 pt. caps and small caps.

13. In general, texts up to seven columns in length are set 8 pt. indent; those longer than seven columns (which with binder line and illustration will run a page or more) are set 8 pt. full measure.

Body type

14. In the body of a text set 8 pt. full measure the use of flush-and-one setting (hanging indention) should be considered in any case in which the beginnings of successive paragraphs have a common element (names in a list, numbers, topics, etc.) that provides pegs from which the paragraphs can hang. In such setting each section must be no more than one paragraph. The flush-and-one form should not be used if the material so set will run more than half a column. Examples:

> Following are the principal points made:
> 1. A demand that make-up men eat all bite-offs.
> 2. A suggestion that all copyreaders read the final edition.
> 3. The proposal that all cablese be eliminated.

> The contributions were listed as follows:
> Afghanistan — Camel trains, four tons of yak butter.
> Belgium—Twenty carloads of coal, 100 carloads of potatoes.

15. Sometimes a topic appears at the beginning of each of several paragraphs followed by a colon or a dash. The topics thus cannot be detached for treatment as independent headings and at the same time may not be suitable for flush-and-one treatment. In such cases the topics should be set fflc or italic or, if

they do not contain too many words, light caps. The choice may depend on which will best contrast with the headings in the text. Another factor may be the fewness of textual headings, which would favor the use of fflc to break up with blackness long stretches of type. Examples:

> **Membership Applications:** Australia, Belgium, Canada, France, Haiti, India, Jamaica.
> **Appropriations:** The Army, the Navy, Commerce, the Interior.

Two-column boxes

16. The introduction, if any, should be set 9 pt. italic full measure and the body 8 pt. roman indent, thus:

> Special to The New York Times
>
> *WASHINGTON, Feb. 15—Following is the text of the Presidential order, issued today, setting up controls:*
> Prices shall be no higher than those obtaining at the close of business on Jan. 31, 1951. Wages shall be no higher than they were for the week ending Dec. 1, 1950.

17. If the subject matter is highlights, flush - and - one setting is usually indicated, with the topics set fflc, followed in each case by a dash, thus:

> **Tariffs**—Revision of duties on hog bristles, zinc ore, magnesium and dental drills.
> **Interstate Commerce**—Strengthening of controls over child labor, bus inspections and safety equipment of railroads.

Basic News Headlines

Following are the basic news headlines used in The New York Times. The size and the style of type are given, with unit counts that represent safe or desired maximums. Sample portions of lines are shown in instances in which the headlines are too large for reproduction here.

K head
9 pt. News Gothic, 24 units.

Drought Threatens Australia

P head
12 pt. Chelt Bold Condensed, 24 units.

Congolese Regime Concurs

G head
8 pt. News Gothic, 17 units.

TEXT OF THE LETTER

D head
12 pt. News Gothic, 23 units.

U.M.W. Sued for $750,000 By Tennessee Coal Concern

M head
14 pt. Cheltenham Bold Italic Condensed, 16 units.

2 CATHOLIC PAPERS DIFFER ON KENNEDY

1-Col. Box head
14 pt. Cheltenham Bold Italic Condensed, 20 units.

School Bus Is Bought With Trading Stamps

C head
Top, 24 pt. Latin Antique Extra Condensed, 14 units.
Bank, 10 pt. News Gothic.

FORD IS SPLITTING ITS STOCK 2 FOR 1

Wider Ownership Is Sought —Dividend Raised to 90c

X head
18 pt. Cheltenham Bold Italic Condensed, 16½ units.

12 Foes of Sukarno Jailed in Indonesia

117

Eloper Wins Right To Visit Wife, 17, At Her L. I. Home

PRESIDENT SEEKS BILLION INCREASE IN DEFENSE FUND

Request for 35-Billion Total Is Indicated in Conference With Congress Leaders

AIR FORCE TO GET MOST

Missiles Also to Be Stressed —Democrats to Support Bipartisan Program

NAVY TO ENLARGE FLEET BY 42 SHIPS IN NEXT 5 MONTHS

Amphibious Craft to Return to Service, Strengthening Troop-Moving Capacity

MUSICIANS STRIKE AT PHILHARMONIC

Concerts Are Unlikely This Week as Talks Break Off in Contract Dispute

NEXT MOVE IS IN DOUBT

Union Asked Men to Accept Terms and Management Refused Mediation

KHRUSHCHEV SEES HOPE FOR PARLEY

Thinks Paris and Bonn Have Softened Their Stands— Poles Add to Forces

R and R-1 heads
Top, 24 pt. Cheltenham Bold Italic, 22 units.
Banks, 14 pt. Cheltenham Bold Italic for R's 2-col. bank and
14 pt. Cheltenham Italic Condensed for R-1's 1-col. bank.

Senate Approves Request For More Arms and Men

Votes Authority for the President to Call 250,000 Reserves—Adds a Billion to Buy Weapons and Equipment

Mountain Hamlet Buried by Avalanche—Toll Is Expected to Rise

R-3 head
Top, two 3-col. lines of same type as R, 33 units.
Bank, same as R-1 bank.

Danish King Conducts Orchestra

Berliners Gather at Barricades Dividing Families and Friends

Mother of Bride Weeps in Red Sector as Her Daughter Is Wed in West— Brother's Plea Goes Unheeded

President Expected to Make Request to Congress for Ten-Year Program

Aides of Stanleyville General Arrive in Leopoldville

U heads

Tops, 24 pt. Bookman Italic, 9½ units to the column. Page 1 U-4's are sometimes set in 30 pt., 8½ units to the column.

Banks, 14 pt. Bookman Italic for three-line 1-col. and 2-col. pyramided banks, and 18 pt. Bookman Italic for 2-col. banks with two lines of the same length, indented both sides.

Hemingway's Will Written in

Widow Gets Estate,
With Instruction to
Provide for Sons

Egrets, Ibises and Geese
Fly to Jamaica Bay Site

Q head

Top, 24 pt. Bookman Italic, 21 units.
Bank, 14 pt. Bookman Italic.

Foreign Aid Objective

Review of Factors Behind President's
Expected Proposals to New Congress

QM head

Top line, 24 pt. Bookman Italic.
Name, 14 pt. Bookman Italic.

Angriest Young Man
John James Osborne

Teacher Suspended for Requiring

Text of Rockefeller Letter

Transcript of President's

ALLIES BID SOVIET

I.C.C. PROPOSES

U. S. MOON ROCKET FIRED

5-col. and 6-col. heads
*Three lines of 36 pt. Century Bold Italic, 26½ units for the
5-col and 32 units for the 6-col.*

SOVIET RESUMING

MOON SHOT

Steel Strike Ends

OFFENSIVE

60 pt., three lines, 25 units.

KENNEDY

Hanger
Top, 24 pt. Latin Antique Extra
Condensed, 14½ units.
Bank, 18 pt. News Gothic.

NEW HAVEN CITED

Agency Asserts Every Passenger Line Is in Same Plight